W9-ASA-622

# The Encounter
## of
## Religions

# The
# of
*A dialogue*

# Religions

*translated by*
PIERRE DE FONTNOUVELLE *with* EVIS MCGREW

*Foreword by*
DIETRICH VON HILDEBRAND

NEW YORK - TOURNAI - PARIS - ROME 1960

# Encounter

*between*

*the West and the Orient*

*with*

an Essay on the Prayer of Jesus

*by Jacques-Albert Cuttat*

DESCLÉE COMPANY

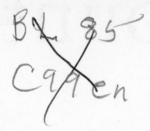

This is a translation of *La Rencontre des Religions* (Paris : Aubier, Éditions Montaigne © 1957)


NIHIL OBSTAT

JAMES F. RIGNEY, S. T. D.

Censor Librorum


IMPRIMATUR     January 19, 1960

✠ FRANCIS CARDINAL SPELLMAN

ARCHBISHOP OF NEW YORK


The nihil obstat and imprimatur are official declarations that a book or pamphlet is free of doctrinal or moral error. No implication is contained therein that those who have granted the nihil obstat and imprimatur agree with the contents, opinions or statements expressed.


Library of Congress Catalog Card Number : 60-10163

*... ut dum visibiliter Deum cognos-
cimus, per hunc in invisibilium
amorem rapiamur.*

(Preface of the Nativity)

To my friend Dietrich von Hildebrand

# TABLE OF CONTENTS

Foreword, by Dietrich von Hildebrand . . . . . . . . 9

Part One : THE ENCOUNTER OF RELIGIONS . . . . . . . . 13

1 Dangers and Advantages of a Comparative Evaluation . . . 15

2 Recollection and Universality . . . . . . . . . . . 19

3 Open Religion . . . . . . . . . . . . . . . . . 23

4 Spiritual Requirements of the Dialogue . . . . . . . . 27
    Creation and Manifestation . . . . . . . . . 27
    Contradiction or Complementarism? . . . . . . 29

5 Interiority and Transcendency . . . . . . . . . . . 35
    The Great Lesson of the Orient . . . . . . . 36
    Extreme Interiority Calls for Monotheistic Transcendency . . . . . . . . . . . . . . . . . 39
    The Development of Buddhism . . . . . . . . 41
    Râmânuja . . . . . . . . . . . . . . . . 42
    Al-Hallâj . . . . . . . . . . . . . . . . 45

6 Equalitarian Correspondence or Spiritual Charity . . . . . 55
    Qualitative Aspect of Religious Time . . . . . . 55
    Incarnation and *Avatâra* . . . . . . . . . . 57
    Buddhist Love *(maitrî)* and Christian Charity *(agapê)* . 58
    Error and Sin; Illusion and Disobedience . . . . 61
    Comments Concerning Ramakrishna . . . . . . 63

7 Conclusion; Antinomic Knowledge, the Opening of Intelligence to Mystery . . . . . . . . . . . . . . . 67
    Knowledge of Faith . . . . . . . . . . . 70
    God Incarnate, Supreme Antinomy and Total Synthesis 72
    The Ambiguity of Traditionalism . . . . . . . 76

Part Two : THE HESYCHAST METHOD OF PRAYER AND ITS SPIRITUAL
              SIGNIFICANCE   IN   THE   BORDERLAND   BETWEEN
              EAST  AND  WEST . . . . . . . . . . . .  85

Introductory remarks . . . . . . . . . . . . . . .  87
1 Analogy-Participation, the  Metaphysical  Basis  of  Hesychast
     Deification or *Theôsis* . . . . . . . . . . . . .  89
          Convergence or Divergence of Nature and Grace . .  91
          Prayer Considered as Inner Eucharist . . . . . .  94

2 The First Phase of *Theôsis* : Enstasy or " Isolation " through
     Interiorization, Eastern Component of Hesychasm . . .  99
          The Search for the Place of the Heart . . . . .  100
          The Contemplative Integration of the Cosmos . . .  101

3 The  Second  Phase  of  *Theôsis* : " Received  Identity, "  the
     Properly Christian Component of Hesychasm . . . .  105
          From the Impersonal Deity to the Living God . . .  105
          The Supraintellectual Essence of Grace . . . . . .  108

4 Dangers and Limits of the Hesychast Method . . . . . .  117
          Extroverted and Introverted Techniques . . . . .  118
          The Twin Menace : Quietism and Voluntarism, Two
               Conjugate Extremes . . . . . . . . . . .  123
          The Danger of Angelism . . . . . . . . .  130
          Can Spiritual Effort be Necessarily Effective? . . . .  135
          Inner Eucharist and Imitation of Christ . . . . . .  139
          Limits of Analogy-Participation . . . . . . .  143
          Conclusion : Value of the Hesychast Method . . . .  147

# FOREWORD

Before reading *The Encounter of Religions*,
I must confess, I knew little about the spiritual world of the
East. From the point of view of my very limited knowledge,
the immanent questions raised by the Orient, its way of
answering basic problems, and even the problems themselves
appeared to me somewhat odd and peculiar. But the reading
of this book changed my view and opened new perspectives
to me; it was a decisive experience, for while reading it,
I discovered more and more that the problems inherent in
the Eastern religions are classical human problems; that here
are involved tendencies to interpret man's metaphysical situation,
and solutions to which man's nature as such is prone. It may
not be presumptuous to assume that many other readers will
share my experience.

The understanding of these problems is invaluable,
because it enables us to recognize subtle dangers — disguised
Eastern influences which have crept into the Christian world.
Even after the self-revelation of God in the Sacred Humanity
of Christ, we still find recurring tendencies to interpret the
relation between man and God in the Eastern spirit. Such is
the case, for instance, in many brands of Christian gnosticism.

The most striking merit of this book, however, is that
it embodies the rare virtue of intellectual charity. True intellectual
charity approaches each great and venerable tradition with
a reverent attitude, seeking to understand it " from within, "
while avoiding the danger of either being caught by it or being
pushed into syncretism.

Intellectual charity essentially requires that we enter,
as it were, into the mentality of the other, but also that we

withdraw from it again, seeking for ourselves nothing but the
objective truth. We fail to be intellectually charitable if we do
not take the trouble to enter into the mentality of the other,
but merely criticize him from without, unready to discover
possible truths in what he is saying. But we also sin against
intellectual charity if we remain in the frame of the other — in
this case, the frame of Eastern religions — without confronting
it with the Christian revelation, if our understanding ends
in yielding. True charity is indissolubly linked with an
unwavering faithfulness to truth, and in this case, to the true
revelation. In the last analysis, we do not take the other person
seriously if we let ourselves be caught by his ideas instead of
letting objective truth be the ultimate judge. We fail to realize
that, in doing so, we betray him.

In the post-Patristic period, Catholics often lacked the
first element of intellectual charity. They did not take the trouble
to penetrate the great traditions of Eastern religions with
a reverent, charitable attitude. They simply pigeonholed these
traditions as pagan idolatry, treating them as one should justly
treat artificial pseudo-religions. Today, on the contrary,
there is a trend among Catholics to fail in the second element
of intellectual charity : the confrontation of everything with
absolute truth, with the revelation of Christ. Through a mis-
interpreted charity, one not only enters into the ideas of other
religions, theories and doctrines, but one remains in them,
one yields to them, one becomes contaminated by them. We
could quote innumerable examples of this modern danger,
the most typical being the Hegelian and sometimes even Marxist
contamination among leftist Catholics.

In this respect, the present book is a spiritual event
in the contemporary world, because Dr. Cuttat abstains equally
from both dangers threatening intellectual charity, and
exemplifies the " true " way of approaching Eastern religions.

But " The Encounter of Religions " is also extremely important and fertile from a purely philosophical point of view, because, in elaborating the classical problems immanent in these Eastern religions, it helps us to unmask many of these trends in modern philosophical theories.

May I end by drawing the reader's attention to the conclusion of this book, which contains, according to an eminent French theologian, " some of the most penetrating pages one can read these days on the significance of prayer [1]. "

**Dietrich von Hildebrand**
Department of Philosophy
Fordham University
December 1959

[1] Michel de Certeau, S.J., *Etudes*, Sept. 1958.

*Part I*

# The Encounter of Religions

# Dangers and Advantages
# of a
# Comparative Evaluation

At first, it may seem that the very idea of confronting two religions implies a totally unwarranted and even contradictory claim, for a comparative evaluation of this type assumes the existence of objective sets of facts facing — so to speak — our intelligence, and of an observer standing outside or even above the object of study. Of all the data available to our consciousness, religion is certainly the field which lends itself least to such an approach *ab extra*. It is obvious that the true nature of human love will inevitably escape us, as long as we consider it only as nonparticipant spectators, and what may be said of this emotion holds true, to an infinitely higher degree, of the essence of all religions. Whether this essence be divine revelation, inspired vision or primordial tradition, it is always experienced as a reality of nonhuman origin, as a suprarational reality irreducible to a discursive judgment. In other words, this essence is experienced as being fundamentally " unobjectifiable, " and therefore accessible only *ab intra*. Religious intuition presupposes a timeless truth which, far from being posited by our intellect or depending on our choice, precedes and determines both these elements. Every true believer in any religion worthy of the name — even if he was converted in adulthood — knows full well that he did not select this particular creed among others, but on the contrary realizes, more and more clearly as he advances in life, that he was chosen by God, " called " from all eternity by Him and toward Him.

There are some who consider the various religions to be as many equivalent paths leading to the same original Truth, from which — in this view — they were all derived through gradual differentiation. But even those who hold this opinion must surely recognize that this Truth underlying all historical religions, this immemorial " Tradition " common to all mankind, was not revealed or manifested as such, and consequently is not directly attainable. They must surely admit that, in order to rediscover this " Lost Word, " one has no choice — there being no other channels open — but to utilize one of the positive and living religions.

This being so, there are two possibilities. Either I observe, with a certain detachment, the whole complex of the various concrete religions, so as to explore them scientifically as so many phenomena, and in that case I am incompetent by definition, since the object of my study becomes not the very essence of religions, but only their anthropological, philosophical, psychological or historical residua or accessories. Or else, my viewpoint being properly religious, I possess the required competence, and I will then necessarily approach the various creeds from and through one of them, namely my own, failing which I would lack both knowledge and authentic spiritual experience.

Is this to say that the science called " Comparative Religion " lacks all religious significance? Yes, if this discipline is reduced to an analysis of the converging and diverging spiritual trends of mankind, an analysis conducted in order to reach an " objective " synthesis of these trends; this kind of synthesis can be nothing but a " reconstruction " based on some largely unconscious philosophical or metaphysical postulate, and therefore can lead only to a purely human and basically nonreligious view of things. No, if we recognize in this comparison an opportunity to deepen and widen our own religion. The present study first proposes to show that the meeting of religions — which constitutes an inevitable corollary of the contemporary confrontation of peoples and civilizations — carries for Christians and Hindus, for Moslems, Buddhists and Taoists, a providential invitation to re-examine and review their own dogma, so as to rediscover implicit or potential dimensions within it, or to open up new horizons, from the vantage point of their own religion.

Traditionalists will no doubt object that such an attitude is colored with subjectivism, since any primacy given to one particular religion implies a judgment of value. They will add that the only way to avoid such partiality is to assert *a priori* the fundamental equality of all mankind's spiritual traditions. To which we will answer that this *a priori* assertion itself implies a judgment of value, or more accurately a petition of principle, which is all the more dangerous for being unconscious. In order to affirm validly the basic equivalence of all religions, it would be necessary to occupy a " metaphysical locus " which would embrace at once the cause and the effect of all religions; to occupy, in other words, a metacosmic point, which would be neither in God who grants revelation, nor in man who receives it; it would be necessary to assume a perspective both prior to and higher than the Creator-creature polarity. This locus, this point and this perspective are manifestly inconceivable and illusory, for the simple reason that there exists absolutely nothing outside this polarity. We are thus inevitably led to wonder whether the postulate of the equivalence of religions may not conceal a Luciferian attempt to withdraw a part of ourselves, namely intelligence, from the meeting between the creature and his Creator. In practice, as a matter of fact, the traditionalists, including those who were originally Christians, by no means escape the inevitable priority of one particular religion; they generally give this primacy to Hinduism, precisely because — one may suspect — it appears to lend itself more than any other system to an avoidance of the exigencies of this confrontation, while still satisfying their religious aspirations.

Be that as it may, the second purpose of the present study is to emphasize the " Promethean " nature of certain temptations inherent in the Meeting of Religions. Since these temptations, like all Satanic interventions, can only arise with the permission of God, we hope to show that their function is to be recognized so as to be overcome, and to be overcome so as to lead us to extract *ex stercore aurum*.

# Recollection
# and
# Universality

During a series of lectures which he gave in 1954 throughout Europe and America, Sir Sarvepalli Radhakrishnan [1], the eminent philosopher, Vice-President of India, and Chancellor of Delhi University, emphasized two particular aspects of Hindu spirituality, which is the only religious system to have maintained perfect continuity over more than four thousand years.

He first referred to man's capacity for self-transcendency. Our ability to discover truth within ourselves, he explained, is the faculty which places us above other living creatures. " Man is at his greatest when he is alone. " We wish to point out that this ability to " enter into oneself, " which Ortega y Gasset called *ensimismamiento*, this inclination to interiority, is typically but by no means exclusively Hindu. It represents, in fact, an element which is common to all mystical systems, including Christianity.

The second aspect of Hindu tradition stressed by the lecturer is what one might call the transcendent universality of the divine. He recalled that, in the words of the *Rig-Veda*, the most ancient text in India, " He (i. e., the Real, the Divine) is one, but the wise men have given him many names. " Other and later texts say : " It is because one may know him in so many different ways that he is addressed under so many names. " The entire spiritual literature of India presents countless variations on this central theme, which Leibnitz called

" *philosophia perennis.* " The Hindu soul is so permeated with this idea that, in the nineteenth century, Ramakrishna put it into practice, as it were, by testing or verifying one after another, not only the various Hindu ways, but also the Islamic way and the Christian way [2]. In order to illustrate this fundamental Hindu belief, Vice-President Radhakrishnan quoted this famous parable of the Moslem mystic Jalâl-ed-Dîn Rûmi : some Hindus exhibited an elephant in a dark hall [3]. Many people gathered to see it, but the light was so dim that they had to feel the animal with their hands, so as to learn what an elephant is like. One man touched the trunk and declared that the beast resembled a waterpipe; another felt an ear and deduced that this pachyderm looked like a fan; a third came up against a leg and maintained that the animal was like a pillar; and still another touched the back and asserted that the elephant was shaped like an enormous throne. So it is also, concluded Rûmi, with those who would describe the divine [4]. There exists no formula capable of embracing the innumerable aspects of the divine's formless essence, which is at once intimate and infinite.

This spiritual viewpoint is indeed most characteristic of the Orient. The Vice-President of India impressed on his audience how intensely conscious his people are of the mysterious, absolutely ineffable, and by the same token omnipresent nature of the Divinity.

*  *
*

[1] In transcribing Sanskrit and Arabic words, we have followed international usage : " j, " " ch " and " sh " are pronounced as in English, and " kh " like the Spanish jota.

[2] In 1886 Ramakrishna, whose influence on Gandhi was considerable, interrupted the practice of Tantrism to live as a Moslem, constantly repeating the name of Allah. In 1893 he became absorbed in the thought of Christ, to the point of eliminating every other consideration from his mind. His

name recalls the seventh *(Rama)* and eighth *(Krishna) avatâra* or descents of Vishnu.

³ According to another version, the elephant was surrounded by blind men.

⁴ Reynold A. Nicholson, trans., *The Mathnawí of Jalálu'ddín Rúmí* (London, Cambridge University Press, 1930), Book III, Vol. IV, p. 71, verses 1259 ff.

# Open Religion

The speaker suggested the following conclusion : according to Arnold Toynbee, mankind is moving toward an Oriental religion, namely Christianity, but in combination with one of the Hindu outlooks. Dr. Radhakrishnan believes that the religion of the future will be a synthesis of Christian religiousness and the central affirmation of the Hindu tradition, which declares that " there are many paths leading to God. "

How should one interpret this rather unexpected conclusion? In his study entitled *Eastern Religions and Western Thought* (London, Oxford University Press, 1939), Dr. Radhakrishnan has made clear his views on the subject. In a chapter devoted to " The Meeting of Religions, " he writes that " there is no worse prejudice than a belief in one's own inerrancy. " And he adds : " Unfortunately, Christian religion inherited the Semitic creed of the ' jealous God ' in the view of Christ as ' the only begotten son of God, ' and so could not brook any rival near the throne. When Europe accepted the Christian religion, in spite of its own broad humanism, it accepted the fierce intolerance which is the natural result of belief in ' the truth once and for all delivered to the saints. ' " Further on in the same chapter, the author asserts that " if the Hindu chants the Vedas . . ., if the Chinese meditates on the Analects, if the Japanese worships the image of Buddha, if the European is convinced of Christ's mediatorship, if the Arab reads the Qur'an in his mosque, and if the African bows down to a fetish, each one of them has exactly the same reason for his particular confidence. " He comments approvingly on Tolstoy, who provided Gandhi with inspiration, for having written : " I have no predilection for Christianity. " He maintains that " the Hindu way is a democratic way " and supports the view that " the final truth, whatever it may be *(sic)*, is the New Testament of every existing faith. " He extols the hope that " the whole of mankind " may one day become " a united people, where Muslim and Christian, Buddhist and Hindu, shall stand together, bound by common devotion, not to something behind but to something ahead . . ., to a great dream of a world society with a universal religion, of which the historical faiths are but branches. "

Is this still an authentically Hindu viewpoint, or perhaps merely a part of Dr. Radhakrishnan's personal philosophy? The following quotations may allow the reader to anwer this question. They represent the opinions of another highly qualified Hindu thinker, Ananda K. Coomaraswamy, who is all the more trustworthy for having devoted his gifts and scholarship to the idea of the fundamental unity of religions. In a critical review [1] of Dr. Radhakrishnan's book, he commends the general intent of this work, and continues in the following terms : " What is perhaps the most disturbing element in the pronouncements of one who occupies the position of the spiritual ambassador of India, is the fact that he himself has manifestly, whether by training or temperament or both, essentially a European rather than an Indian mentality. He accepts without hesitation the current academic notion of human ' progress, ' with the correlative ' development ' of ' systems ' of ' religious philosophy, ' not realizing what India has known so well, that there are things to which the historical method, valid only for the classification of facts and not for the elucidation of principles, does not apply. " And further on : " It seems to us that Radhakrishnan has forgotten what it is to be a Hindu, and has become an ' Orientalist, ' and that is unfair to a majority of his readers, who cannot go directly to the sources for themselves. " As far as Coomaraswamy is concerned, " . . . it is clear that Radhakrishnan would reject the whole idea of a superhuman origin of the orthodox tradition, together with the corresponding Christian concept of revelation, and that for this reason it does not occur to him to correlate the doctrine of . . . the ' timelessness of the Dhamma ' with the Christian dogma of the eternity of the Divine Word. " Coomaraswamy does not hesitate to say that " Radhakrishnan is thoroughly un-Indian (as well as un-Christian) when he speaks of ' our strong dislike of monasticism ' . . . and enthusiasm for what he calls an ' open religion. ' " He draws this conclusion : " Modern tolerance is to a very large extent a symptom of indifference to spiritual truth or error, or of the conviction that the truth can never be known. "

It is therefore clear that the " great dream " of a " universal religion, " which constitutes, so to speak, the synthetic flower of a tolerant evolutionism, raises objections from within the Orient itself. The humanistic aspiration toward a gradual merging of existing creeds runs against the spiritual sensitivity of both hemispheres, and it is unable to quote any sacred writing of the East or the West as authority because, in the final analysis, it reckons without God. Is this to say that there exists no solution to the pressing and inevitable problem of the " Encounter of Religions? " Is each religion condemned to remain isolated behind its own sacerdotal curtain? Is the dialogue between religions meaningless, as Karl Barth maintained? We are convinced that the opposite is true.

The outstanding contribution made by Dr. Radhakrishnan — the first Oriental to hold a professorship at Oxford — is precisely that of having opened this dialogue, together with other great thinkers such as Coomaraswamy, René Guénon, Frithiof Schuon, Rudolf Otto, Mircea Eliade, Henri de Lubac, Jacques Maritain, Olivier Lacombe, Louis Gardet, Louis Massignon, Miguel Asín Palacios, Louis Renou, Paul Masson-Oursel, Louis de la Vallée-Poussin, Leopold Ziegler, and Teitaro

Suzuki. The merit of Dr. Radhakrishnan lies less in his conclusions than in the fact that he placed this Meeting on a higher plane than that of Occultism, high enough so that we are now enabled to pursue the Dialogue in another direction.

\* \*
\*

[1] Also entitled " Eastern Religions and Western Thought, " *The Review of Religion* (Columbia University Press), Vol. VI, No. 2 (January, 1942), pp. 129-46.

# Spiritual
# Requirements
# of the Dialogue

# 4

Neither Radhakrishnan nor Coomaraswamy seem to have realized that the modern concept of " progress, " acclaimed by the former and rejected by the latter, is but the secularization of Judeo-Christian eschatology. This secularization reduces to earthly and historical proportions a superterrestrial and transhistorical outlook, which appeared with the Hebraic religion and is inseparably linked to monotheism, i. e., to the revelation of the personal God. For the first time in the recorded history of religions, the Old Testament considers the universe as a reality willed as such by the one almighty God, and not merely tolerated by Him.

### Creation and Manifestation.

Indeed, the Abrahamic or monotheistic revelation introduced a vision of the world as creation, whereas Antiquity and the Orient saw it as manifestation. Creation, being a deliberate act, implies as its absolute origin a personal Being, an increate Maker. On the other hand, the universe considered as manifestation is a necessary emanation, and therefore does not assume a creative will as absolute origin, but rather an impersonal metaphysical Principle, a " nonmanifested " infinite. Today, half of mankind (Jews, Christians and Moslems [1]) professes " monotheism, " which is, incidentally, a most unsatisfactory designation, since it expresses only the fact that God is " One " and seems to contrast with " polytheism "

(multiplicity of gods), whereas actually it is the reverse of
" impersonalism. " The monotheistic God is not just " one
and only " — the Absolute of other religions shares in this
particular attribute —, but He is also personal in His absolute
essence itself. He is the Absolute revealing itself as Person.

The other half of the earth's population belongs to the
specifically Oriental religions [2], and to those known as
" primitive. [3] " As far as this spiritual hemisphere is concerned,
the divine Absolute is impersonal or suprapersonal in its
ultimate, transcendent reality, and personal only in certain
of its relative features, or in its immanent manifestations. In
this view, the universe and God form a kind of totality, which
is unmanifested in its essence but manifested in its effects, or
more accurately a Bi-Unity at once infinite and finite, eternal
and temporal, according to the standpoint from which it is
considered [4]. This half of mankind would not therefore conceive
of the world as a created reality, i. e., as having first been
" invented " out of nothing by a pre-existent God and then
gradually brought into being, but rather as the perpetual
reflection of a coexistent Eternity, or as an immemorial, but
fleeting and imperfect, " image " of a blissful and impassive
Reality.

As manifestation, the universe represents inevitable
deterioration, but as creation, it is providential growth. Devoid
of reality outside their unmanifested source, the Taoist " Wheel
of things, " the Buddhist " Circle of existence " *(Samsâra)*,
the " cycles of manifestation " of Brahma (divine " magician "
of *Maya*, the " universal illusion "), and the Greek *Cosmos*
are in themselves illusive and " deifugal; " freely endowed
by the Maker with a reality of its own, the Biblical universe
possesses a divine vocation. For this reason, to the reversible
and cyclic time of non-Biblical cosmologies, to the perpetual
alternation of the " days and nights of Brahma " — in which
the cosmic process is an inevitable removal from the divine

—, Abrahamic revelation has substituted irreversible, linear and theocentric time, in which Creation as such, conceived and prefigured in the " six days " of Genesis, is on the contrary a progressive ascent, through man, toward the Creator. Inaugurating the valorization of time, the Old Testament revealed the world as history [5].

When this valorization of time is stripped of its trans-historical or eschatological finality and deviates toward mere intrahistorical and earthly ideals, however, it loses all justification and turns into Utopian progressism : *corruptio optimi pessima*. The East would have been spared such worship of the temporal future, the worst kind of idolatry, if this aberration had not been imported from the modern West; and perhaps Dr. Radhakrishnan would have rejected this ideology, if he had recognized in it a profanation of the design revealed by the " jealous God " whom he repudiates. Instead of cherishing the great dream of an " open religion, " perhaps he would have raised the crucial question which the two hemispheres must face in their religious encounter : are the monotheistic outlook of the West and the metaphysical perspective of the East compatible? If not, if the personal God precludes all impersonal aspects of the divinity, how can one explain the astonishing convergence of the Western and Eastern mystical systems? If on the other hand we are confronted with equally authentic spiritual dimensions, how can we reconcile them without falling into the triteness of agnostic relativism, the abstract universality of religious syncretism, or the ambiguities of " traditionalism " (itself problematical and, in the final analysis, syncretistic)? We will briefly state the terms of this vital problem.

### Contradiction or Complementarism?

The fact that these two spiritual " dimensions " of mankind are the only authentic ones rules out the possibility of synthetizing them into a third, which would be their common denominator. Moreover, the fact that both are authentic prevents us from reducing either one to the other. Finally, their mere apposition would contradict the transcendent unity of God, as well as the immanent unity of human nature. This unity requires that we look upon the two dimensions in question as being fundamentally complementary and, therefore, that one be subordinate to the other. In simple logic, we are thus led to consider which of these viewpoints is capable of including the other without absorbing or mutilating it. The problem is to join them in a complementarism which would not be merely horizontal, like that of the sexes — this would bring us back to syncretism —, but rather vertical, like that of nature and Grace. This requirement arises because our dilemma is in the spiritual realm, and because there dwells in every man an image of God ordered to His likeness, a supernatural vocation.

In the following pages, we will endeavor to show, without leaving the path of logic or resorting to the authority of the dogma, that the metaphysical perspective cannot subordinate the monotheistic viewpoint without eventually depriving it of its essential elements — personal transcendency, gratuitousness of Grace, supreme value of love —, whereas monotheistic revelation is capable of embracing the Eastern perspective, in such a way that the true essence of the latter is not only preserved, but actually heightened. As we shall see, this can and must be the outcome, by virtue of what the Greek Fathers called the co-operation or " synergy " of nature and Grace. The medieval sayings, *gratia supponit naturam eamque perficit* or *gratia naturam non tollit, sed perficit*, express this same synergetic and providential complementarism [6].

The prime and difficult requirement of a comparative study of religions is the *epokhê*, or phenomenological reduction, i. e., the suspension of judgment — including the judgment of existence — in front of the thing itself, in order to let it speak [7]. Religious *epokhê* does not imply surrendering the substance of our convictions, but merely " placing in parentheses " their incidental modalities. It is a matter of provisionally eliding or " reducing " the extradivine concomitants of our own religious perspective, and in particular all philosophical and psychological apriorisms. The essence of our convictions, far from being abandoned, subsists in implicit and latent form, and opens to new spiritual vistas. Being convinced that every pure yearning after the Sacred contains as such a certain sacred element, and therefore that it receives some kind of divine answer, we will formulate as follows the Golden Rule which applies in matters of Comparative Religion : the more deeply I go into my own religion, the more I become capable of penetrating and assimilating the core, the really positive content, of other religious perspectives. This attitude seems to us the only one capable of providing a " sacred ground " for the inter-religious meeting. This " sacred ground " is essential, if the encounter is to be (1) a religious, and not merely a philosophical, psychological, or historical one, and (2) a true meeting, i. e., a dialogue and not a monologue.

Here is a negative illustration of the above. In medieval India and China, there occurred, simultaneously and without apparent connection, a rapid extension of *bhakti* (the way of mystical love), which had previously been overshadowed by *jnâna* (the way of knowledge). Both in Brahmanism and in Buddhism, there arose a concurrent tendency to abandon the primacy of knowledge over love as way toward God, and to subordinate " withdrawal within oneself, " or Gnostic " enstasy, " to adoration of the transcendent Lord, or Bhaktic " ecstasy. " This extension coincided roughly with the beginning of the Christian era. The major significance of this coincidence appears to have escaped Western orientalists and missionaries, as well as Orientals interested in the Christian West. We believe that it was overlooked by the former because they are blinded by the extraneous concomitants of the Incarnation — Western civilization, individualistic psychology, Aristotelian philosophy, political power, etc. —, and therefore fail to recognize that Christ's Grace can directly manifest itself anywhere and in anyone. And we are of the opinion that this coincidence escaped the latter because they were so intent on their controversy between the proponents of "ways of knowledge" *(Shivaites, Jnânis)* and those of "ways of love" *(Vishnuites, Bhaktas)* that they failed to recognize fully the providential and complementary nature of these various ways, and because they attempted to reduce one category to the other, particularly the ways of love to the ways of knowledge; these Orientals have not perceived that love of the inaccessible Lord does not exclude knowledge of the Self *(Atmâ)*, but instead implies and crowns this knowledge, and that such is precisely the deep significance of the historical evolution which we have just considered. In practice, the West is not fully aware of the omnipresence of the Word [8]. And the East has not yet explicitly discovered that the extreme interiority of the Spirit culminates in the extreme transcendency of the Creator. It may be helpful to examine these points more closely.

*       *
*

[1] According to the latest statistics, these three religions have a combined membership of 1.1 billion.

[2] Hinduism, Buddhism, Jainism, Confucianism, Taoism and Shintoism, with a combined membership of one billion.

[3] 121 million human beings fall into this category. The rest of mankind, numbering about 300 million, includes the secondary religions and those individuals who are without any kind of religious affiliation.

[4] We choose to avoid the disparaging term of Pantheism (" everything is God ") because the East is perfectly aware of the divine transcendency, and in no way deifies nature as such. A much better world would be Panentheism (" everything is in God ") which, instead of culminating in the Personal God, like Monotheism, ends in what Rudolf Otto calls " Theopantism " (" God is everything, " He is the only Reality).

The Divinity of Theopantism, such as the Vedic Brahma or the Allâh of Plotinizing Sufism, has sometimes been called " superpersonal. " But this Divinity is in fact impersonal, since an absolutely solitary Person, devoid of any alterity or intersubjective space, inevitably resolves itself into an undifferentiated oneness. When applied to the monotheistic God, the adjective " superpersonal " is as contrary as would be the term " super-absolute. "

5 The trail-blazing works of Pierre Teilhard de Chardin, S.J., have further developed this Biblical valorization of History, and have extended it to the spatial and particularly temporal dimensions of the world, as it appears to present-day scientists. According to that eminent thinker, the " vitalization " of matter, the " hominization " of life, and the caritative, intersubjective and social " personalization " of man constitute as many phases in the growth of a cosmic Consciousness which is already latent in matter, and which never ceases to gain in concentration and depth. This process is carried on, first on the level of the " Biosphere, " through paradoxically concurrent diversification and unification, then on the human level of the " Noosphere, " where the cosmic Consciousness acquires " personality " and " universality. " Taken as a phenomenon scientifically observable in its duration or evolution, the total universe — the origin of which through creation Father Teilhard de Chardin, as a naturalist, neither affirms nor denies — therefore tends toward a kind of gradual " involution, " by the very fact that it converges increasingly toward a focus of attraction which is both final and pre-existent, " not generated, but generating. " The author calls this transcendent focus of attraction the " Omega Point " and identifies it with Christ, the " Great Christ " of which Saint Paul says that He will, in the fullness of time, submit the entire creation and Himself to the Father, so " that God may be all in all " (I *Cor.* 15 : 25-28).

To be sure, the futurism of the author overlooks the gloomy scriptural prophecies concerning the end of the world. He seems, at times, to place eternal life in the temporal future, to forget that the possibility of evil (particularly moral evil) necessarily increases with the growth of freedom, and to believe, like Origen, in the ultimate resorption of hell into the " cosmic Body " of Christ. We are of the opinion, however, that these shortcomings, although real enough, are quite corrigible, and that the theories of this eminent geologist and paleontologist allow us to avert other and even graver dangers. They dispel the illusion that the humanity of the Creating Word is incompatible with a universe in which man seems lost among the atoms, species and galaxies, and where the monotheistic faith appears reduced to the status of one creed among many others. In reading his fervent *Messe sur le Monde* (see *La Table Ronde*, June 1956 issue, page 26), one can but rejoice to see a scientist widen his Christian faith to match the scale of a prodigiously expanding and ever more enigmatic universe, and to witness this faith growing into an intimate experience of the personal omnipresence of the Word, " Who was in the world, by Whom the world was made, and Whom the world (e. g., as seen by so many scientists) did not recognize, " Whose workings, in this new light, appear at once more mysterious and less questionable than one had ever believed or dared to hope.

It is remarkable that such an outstanding naturalist, in order to make the data of his scientific specialty more intelligible, was led to explain, not man through the evolution of the universe, but rather, the evolution of the universe through man, because everything in the universe leads to man. It is remarkable also, in order to interpret the psychophysiological modalities of the emergence of life and man, that he required the monotheistic concept of person, incommunicable and imperishable thanks to its specific interiority open to Him Who is Absolutely Other (see below, page 50, Footnote 12. Cf. particularly *L'Univers Personnalisant*, in *Le Phénomène Humain*, Paris, Editions du Seuil, 1955, pp. 289 ff).

[6] On this subject, the reader is referred to *Liturgie Cosmique, Maxime le Confesseur*, by Hans Urs von Balthasar (Paris, Aubier, 1947), and in particular to the chapter entitled " Synthèse Christologique, " pp. 150 ff.

[7] On the religious *epokhê*, see G. Van der Leeuw : *La religion dans son essence et ses manifestations, Phénoménologie de la Religion* (French translation, Payot, 1955), and in particular the highly significant Epilogue (pp. 654-79).

[8] " The rays of the Word ", said Saint Hilary, " are eternally ready to shine wherever, in all simplicity, the windows of the soul are opened. " (commentary on Psalm 118, XII, 5; quoted by Henri de Lubac, S.J., *Amida*, p. 307.)

Through the Spirit, we rise toward the
Son; through the Son, we rise toward the
Father.

Saint IRENAEUS
(Adv. Haereses, V, 36, 2)

# Interiority
## and
## Transcendency

5

Interiority predominates in Eastern
religions, and transcendency in monotheistic religions. We
say "predominates," because these are two complementary
approaches. Both are essential, and as soon as one eliminates
the other, religion ceases to be authentic. When, for instance,
the idea of transcendency supplants interiority, contemplation
degenerates into ritualism or fideism, and piety into moralism.
When, on the other hand, interiority asserts itself to the extent
of absorbing or overlooking transcendency, contemplative life
degenerates into quietism or Gnosticism, and active life into
amoralism [1]. " The Kingdom of Heaven is within you, " and yet,
" None is good but one, that is God " (*Mk*. 10 : 18). " Faith, "
says Boethius, " lies midway between two heresies. "

In *Eastern Religions and Western Thought*, Radhakrishnan
quotes several disgraceful statements made by Christian
missionaries and theologians. Here is one which brings to
mind the parable of the beam and the mote : " ... there is
little in either Hinduism or Islam which can resist the irreligious
influence of economic and psychological determinism " (from

the report of an Evangelical commission for Christian education in India). Or again, here is the opinion of Karl Barth, who believed that any attempt to discover some great value in other religions " should be completely abandoned. " Such lack of inner response to unfamiliar spiritual experiences, far from bearing witness to Christian faith, shows a strange insensitivity to the contemplative aspects of that very faith. Louis Gardet rightly reminds us that, " if Christian theology currently teaches that the life of Grace is possible outside the visible structure of the Church . . ., " this implies, for the faithful of other religions, " the corresponding possibility of a truly mystical life [2]. " The cure for our spiritual exclusivism, however, is not tolerance, but interiorisation of the Christian revelation. Precisely herein resides the " pedagogical " value — in the sense of the divine *paidagogia* of Saint Irenaeus — of the Meeting of Religions. This value is providential for us (before being providential for others) : with increasing clearness, the originality, the beauty and the depth of Oriental spirituality, so close to monotheistic contemplation through its sense of the absolute value of the Sacred, presents itself to Western man as a mirror which invites and helps him to rediscover forgotten aspects of his own revelation, to develop some of its implicit modalities and, above all, to re-emphasize certain neglected demands of the Christian vocation [3].

### The Great Lesson of the Orient.

Among the Hindu teachings of this kind, there is one which we, together with Olivier Lacombe and Louis Gardet, consider more characteristic and more important than universality, which is, as a matter of fact, only a recent element of Hinduism. We refer to the exceptional powers of concentration of the Hindu contemplative. A product of the immemorial tradition of *Yoga* (so often distorted by occultists), concentration, i. e., mastery over the soul's natural tendency toward dispersion, has encouraged an unprecedented development of contemplative interiority. We say contemplative rather than psychological, and interiority rather than introspection, because the manner in which Radhakrishnan defines man, as image of God, might cause misunderstanding in this respect : " A principle of subjectivity irreducible to objectivity. " It can be seen that this eminent philosopher's definition follows Western idealism, rather than the Hindu doctrine of the *Atmâ* (the " Self ", or supraindividual immanence of God in man) [4]. " It is not a matter of descending into the depths of subjectivity, " specifies Louis Gardet in this connection, " but on the contrary of transcending subjectivity, experienced as such, or of reaching beyond it toward an absolute of which subjectivity is the indication. [5] " Hindu concentration *(dharanâ* and *dhyâna)* sets the total (psycho-physical) consciousness into concentric motion toward the ontological root of intelligence and will. Far from descending into the subconscious, it moves in the opposite direction; it aspires, by definition, to surmount the subject-object duality, so as to achieve a transconscious state *(samâdhi)*, the spiritual locus of which (the Hindu *Buddhi*) is none other than the *noûs* (" contemplative intellect ") of the Greek Fathers and the " fine point of the soul " of Saint Augustine.

One would singularly underestimate the transcendency of God, if one were to believe that this transcendency is accessible only from the peripheral and superficial (i. e., the subjective and individual) modalities of our consciousness. The opposite is true. The more consciousness grows deep and centered (that is to say, detached from the ego), the more it becomes permeable to the presence of the transcendent Divinity. The pedagogical value of the admirable examples of spiritual interiority which our Oriental brothers give us is not confined to what Max Scheler considers the dominant religious feature of the Orient, the " affective union with the Cosmos, " which has also been called " universal sympathy " (Plotinus) and " cosmic charity " (René Guénon). Neither does this value reside merely in the fact that Hindu techniques of concentration (retraction of the senses, control over mental fluctuations) disclose inner riches which remain generally unsuspected in the extroverted West. Contact with the contemplative East teaches something more. To start with, it illustrates the primacy, in the spiritual order, of implementation over theory, of the " operative " over the " speculative, " and consequently of intuition over postulate. Eastern contact revives this fundamentally Christian truth, which is too often forgotten, by furnishing it with " extrinsic proofs, " as Saint Thomas said in a similar connection. In addition, this contact widens the field of what we call mystical theology, by reminding us that the aspiration to the Divine is a normal one, normal not in the sense of frequent or easy, but of inherent in the human vocation, as opposed to " spiritual luxury. " As evidenced by the conversion or the return to Christianity (or to a more intense life in Christ) of several distinguished Orientalists [6], the East fully demonstrates to us that systematic, conscious and deliberate recollection constitutes an effective and legitimate method of making the soul more obedient to the " motions of the Holy Spirit. " Moreover, since Hindu methods of concentration seek above all to break the " circuit " between consciousness and the lower psychic activity, the study of these methods helps to distinguish the suprapsychic and preconceptual (but certainly not anticonceptual) essence of faith. Familiarity with the East protects the idea of faith against the temptation of fideism and frees it from the pernicious psychoanalytical confusion between the realm of the psyche and that of the spirit. In other words, a study of the East expands the concept of *via purgativa*. In so doing, it adds to the moral significance of " repentance, " the contemplative connotation of its Greeks equivalent *metanoia*, which actually denotes a " sudden intellectual change, " a return toward Adamic integrity [7]. Familiarity with the East consequently tends to reconcile anthropocentrism and theocentrism, interiority and transcendency, those two mystical poles whose complementary nature is so forcefully brought out in the famous Patristic saying : " The Holy Spirit is even more inward to my soul than I am myself [8]. "

### *Extreme Interiority Calls for Monotheistic Transcendency.*

These words allow us to perceive the providential role which Biblical monotheism, in turn, plays in relation to Oriental religions. Interiority is ordered to transcendency — as the base of a structure is ordered to its summit —, but it would be wrong to conclude that the former necessarily culminates in the latter, by the sheer effect of its own impetus; interiorization prepares the meeting with Grace, but does not produce it. More than an inner ascent toward God, monotheism implies a descent of God toward man, a divine initiative received as such, better received assuredly (except for special charisms) in the Godlike center of consciousness than at its surface, but nevertheless " received, " and not spontaneous or regained.

In this instance, the significance of the " Meeting " consists less in clarifying than in opening new horizons. Here is the rest of the quotation from Louis Gardet given under Footnote 7 : " Will man continue this movement through his own resources? Perhaps, if the goal reached by him is on his own level and scale of existence, even though he may call this goal God. But if this end-term transcends him absolutely, will it not be necessary, in the course of his movement of interiorization, for him to go out to meet the Other and wait for Him to reveal His mystery, speak to him and give him His love, as Friend to friend, though he might not even know the Friend's name? " Monotheistic mysticism neither overlooks nor rules out " enstatic " self-knowledge, as the fideists imagine, but neither does it end in this knowledge, as the Gnostics have always wished it to do. Monotheistic mysticism converts this self-knowledge into an " outward movement toward the

Other, " into a supraintellectual *ek-stasis*, a love which
" surpasses all knowledge. " The end-point of the concentric
and cognitive movement toward the ontological core of oneself,
which Orientals place symbolically at the very center of the
heart, is seen to be, in the monotheistic perspective, the starting
point of a new movement, an open and caritative movement
toward the depths of God [9]. The deeper is the enstatic
recollection, the more complete and authentic will also be the
contemplative love. It is true that most pseudo-mystical
aberrations denounced by the masters of contemplation can
be traced to an *ek-static* movement which is premature,
superficial and anthropomorphous, because it does not proceed
from the innermost center of the soul. But it is even truer
that, deepest within the most holy of men, there can be no
innermost essence which God does not transcend infinitely.
The meeting of monotheism with the Orient does not only
bring face to face doctrines or experiences — as Radhakrishnan
appears to believe —, but it also confronts the personal God
and the human person.

The personal God, creator and judge of all men, is the
same God whose " invisible attributes, eternal power and
divinity, " according to Saint Paul, " are, from the creation
of the world, understood by the things that are made "
(*Rom*. 1: 20). The Gentiles of both East and West were certainly
not able to know God through their own efforts, but " that
which is known of God is manifest in them, for God has
manifested it unto them " (ibid., 19). The " world-wide "
outlook which modern civilization increasingly forces on human
consciousness invites us to extend to the Orient the Pauline
concept of the Gentiles [10].

Christ, the " God who became man so that man might
become God " (Saint Athanasius), is the complete union of
full interiority and absolute transcendency. We have already
seen that the historical perspective, i. e., the valorization of

time, appeared with the monotheistic vision, according to which the universe admits of a "theocentric" orientation consonant with the "Plan" of its Creator. Christianity, in turn, revealed the "Christocentric" nature of this trajectory. It is consequently incumbent upon us to include the religious past and present of the Orient in our vision of the world as a "Sacred History," and to ask ourselves in what sense the destiny of Oriental souls is also Christocentric. Long years of service in Buddhist lands developed in one Jesuit missionary the conviction that a fervent Buddhist is "often closer than we realize to the One Who is the goal of the salvific hope which He Himself has kindled in the depths of our hearts [11]." If it be true that it is the "Grace given us in Christ Jesus before the times of the world" (II *Tim.* 1 : 9) which is germinating within the immemorial mystical continuity of the Orient, is it not the duty of present-day Christians, placed as they are at the crossroads of religions, to become aware of that which, in the other hemisphere also entrusted to the Son by the Father, foreshadows the Word and leads, without naming It, to His mystical Body? The ability to recognize the "Face of the Father" in every creature who catches a glimpse of Him is a function of our own permeability to His omnipresent Divinity. "I was a stranger and you received Me not, I was naked and you clothed Me not [12] ... "

We believe that the following examples will illustrate this "history" of the presence of the personal God to non-Christian hearts.

## The Development of Buddhism.

Our first example is taken from the history of Buddhism. The Buddha preached his doctrine in northern India during the sixth century B.C. In its original form, Buddhism was an asceticism of *nirvâna* (the extinction of the desire to exist),

based on man's " own power " and making no mention of God.
Toward the beginning of the Christian era, Buddhist compassion
*(karûna)* gradually came to the fore, and with it the desire to
gain deliverance " for the sake of others. " As it spread through
China (seventh century A.D.) and Japan (eleventh century),
Buddhism extolled, over against man's " own power, " the
need for the " power of the Other. " Amidism, or " Buddhism
of faith, " which includes half the population of Japan, finally
became a religion of confident surrender to the eternal *Amida*
Buddha (" Infinite Light " or " Infinite Life "), founded on
the efficacy of His Vow that all men, righteous or sinners, who
invoke his name even once, will be born again in the " Land
of the Pure. " In order to account for this " theocentric "
transmutation of an acseticism of nothingness which seemed
to exclude God, we can hardly escape the following question :
in the light of the universal " Sacred History, " what does
the sudden appearance of the " Buddhism of faith " signify?
It is merely the idolatrous divinization of a compassionate
man? Would it not be more " religious, " i. e., more in
conformity with the God-like nature of the human soul, to
recognize in this evolution an implicit adoration of the personal
God, an adoration kindled unawares by an " awakened " man
(the *Buddha*), propagated by the articulate enthusiasm of his
sermons, and nurtured over more than a thousand years through
the imitation of his serene and radiant " inward gaze, " an adoration mysteriously received by the unknown but true God [13]?

### Râmânuja.

The answer of the personal God appears more clearly
in the case of the eleventh century Hindu mystic Râmânuja,
who brought full theological maturity to the " Bhaktic "
devotion, which we have already mentioned on several occasions.
His exceptional interest lies in the fact that he exalts the absolute
transcendency of the divine Lord *(Ishvara)* as Person, after

having experienced the intellective (or "*jnânic*") way of the
famous Shankarâcharya, the undisputed master and eminent
protagonist of complete interiorization. In the *jnânic* view,
Brahma (the divine Absolute) not only surpasses the relative
reality of the world; he is the only reality, so real that the mere
fact of considering anything — be it the world, other men,
or oneself — as being outside Him or distinct from Him, can
only be the result of ignorance, and therefore, in the final analysis,
an error pure and simple, although a hereditary and inveterate
one. The phenomenal world is *mâya* : a sorrowful illusion
superimposed on the exclusive and blessed reality of Brahma,
a collective hallucination which vanishes as soon as we become
aware that, in our innermost essence *(âtmâ)*, we are and have
never ceased to be Brahma. Consequently, it is not a matter
of gaining our identity with Him, since it was never lost, but
of perceiving this identity and recovering its memory. This
is achieved by dissolving every illusion created by the erroneous
distinction between " knowing subject " and " known object. "
We must become thoroughly imbued with our divine identity,
to the point of erasing the ultimate duality, itself an illusion,
between God and creature. At the conclusion of a long and
agonizing spiritual crisis, Râmânuja discovered why he was
left unsatisfied by " absolute nondualism, " the extreme and
purely intellectual interpretation of the traditional equation
$âtmâ = Brahma$ [14]. He gradually recognized that the ascetic,
in his effort to go beyond the " God-creature " polarity
and to become completely absorbed in Brahma, eventually
reaches Him as undifferentiated Absolute, but also loses Him
as transcendent Lord : it is impossible to deny Him as " totally
Other " without by the same token losing His presence.
Râmânuja saw clearly that Shankarâcharya, to the extent that
he inwardly bridged the interval between the divine and the
human, also eliminated the reciprocity required by the Meeting,
abolished the distance implied by Love, and closed the abyss
implied by God's mercy. Whereas Shankara saw in the total

interiorization of God an expansion of intelligence beyond
all devotional duality, beyond the mere lordly aspect of Brahma,
Râmânuja experienced this interiorization as actually being
a restriction of consciousness to the intelligible " portion "
of God's omnipresence. In Râmânuja's opinion, this restriction
is in fact connoted by the word *kaivalya* (literally " isolation ",
" detachment ", " stripping of all alterity "), attribute of the
" delivered " man. To Shankara, this technical term of Hindu
spirituality meant aloneness beyond the " qualified " Brahma
(identical with Ishvara, the Lord); but to Râmânuja, the same
term means isolation short of Brahma, indivisibly " qualified "
*(saguna)* and " nonqualified " *(nirguna)*, inseparably Lord and
supreme Reality. In a masterly vision, Râmânuja discovered
that contemplative intellectualism excludes love, while
contemplative love, on the contrary, is capable of including
the intellect : love takes away from the intellect only its
congenital propensity to close over its " divine Object " and
rest in itself, but on the other hand love imparts to the intellect
its own open impulse. " Bhaktic " communion, indeed, always
remains open to the free person-to-Person communication,
because it implies " the mediation of two freedoms, that of the
creature, who may elect to keep ' to itself, ' and that of Grace,
which freely chooses its friends [15]. " How did Râmânuja succeed
in reconciling this mutual freedom inherent in Love with the
Vedic dogma " *âtmâ is Brahma,* " according to which man
coincides with God in his own essence, i. e., by right? How
did he render plausible the belief that the same Brahma who
constitutes our fundamental reality is at the same time the
inaccessible Lord, the sovereignly free Person [16]? To show
that this antinomy is not contradictory, Râmânuja utilizes
an analogy neglected by Shankara, one which is more Christian
than Hindu in structure (this detail itself is highly significant) :
that of the union between body and soul. This analogy allows
him to affirm that man and God are neither heterogeneous
— so that *âtmâ* is fundamentally *Brahma* —, nor identical, but

" united. " We are a " mode " of Brahma, said Râmânuja, not as a drop of water is to the ocean, but as the body is to the soul : the physical world and the world of spirits between them make up the " body of Brahma. "


## *Al-Hallâj.*

Finally, there is a dazzling quality about the answer of the personal God in the life of the great Moslem mystic and martyr Al-Hallâj, who in 922 A.D. was hanged (or crucified, according to another version) in Baghdad, for having proclaimed that his supernatural love had transfigured him into Allah. One cannot understand the violence of this reaction, which would be inconceivable in the setting of India, without placing it against the background of Islamic orthodoxy. At the opposite extreme from Hinduism, official (or exoteric) Islam tends to consider God as being, not only inaccessible, but also beyond any human participation, as having revealed His Word without revealing Himself. This " fideistic " atmosphere which surrounded Al-Hallâj allows us to realize the scandal caused by his mystical exclamations and " theopathic locutions, " of which we will now quote some of the most famous : " I am the Truth; " " I am the One I love, and the One I love has become myself; we are two spirits united in a single body; " " With my whole being I have embraced all Your love, O my Holiness; " " The greeting I give him is pure metaphor; my salutation, in reality, goes from me to myself. " These exclamations were all the more compromising because Al-Hallâj found in Christ, more than in Mohammed, his true master and his example, as witnessed by a litany which he is said to have improvised during his martyrdom [17]. " Praised be God, " he said in one of his best-known verses, " Who has revealed in His Humanity the mystery of His radiant Divinity. " On the point of being executed, he exclaimed that he preferred his enemies to his defenders, because "my enemies condemn me for love of Thee, while my friends defend me for love of myself," and he died calling God's mercy on the executioners who were cutting off his hands and feet. To the two "mono-theistic dimensions" which we have already encountered in other non-Christian traditions — intuition of the gratuity of Grace (Buddhism of faith), and intimate communion with the personal and transcendent God (Râmânuja) —, we can now add a third : the crucifying aspect of unitive love, together with the intercessory value of the suffering implied by this love [18].

Like Râmânuja, Al-Hallâj proclaimed the primacy of Love only after having himself explored the way of a purely intellective interiorization of God, which so many other Sufis (Moslem mystics), on the contrary, place above the way of love. Both Râmânuja and Al-Hallâj call isolation or aloneness (*kaivalya* in Sanskrit, *tajrîd* in Arabic) the culmination of enstasy in the experience of "fulfilled possession," which is a product of total absorption or "extinction" in the divine Absolute (*nirvâna* in Sanskrit, *el-fanâ* in Arabic). But while the Hindu considers enstasy as a distinct path, legitimate though inferior, the Arab sees in it the point of departure of unitive love (*tawhîd*), and warns us that this first stage, far from being sufficient in itself, turns into a "Luciferian" temptation when the mystic remains at this level and is content with it [19]. Al-Hallâj overcame the temptation to rest in Gnostic enstasy and, precisely because he recognized that this state constitutes a temptation, he was able to extend farther than his Hindu spiritual brother the open impulse, the outward movement toward the depths of the "totally Other." Beyond the "unification of oneself in oneself" of Gnostic enstasy, beyond also the "unification of oneself in God" of Bhaktic ecstasy, Moslem mysticism — and particularly that of Al-Hallâj — places what it calls the "oneness of God proclaimed in the soul by God himself." At this third and supreme level appears the influx of divine gratuity : the outlook is reversed, and we pass — in Christian terminology — from acquired contemplation to infused contemplation. When he says, for instance " Between Thou and I, there is an ' I am ' which grieves me, " Al-Hallâj aspires, not to bridge the theandric distance, but on the contrary to make himself permeable to its infinity, to open himself to a will which, by its very inaccessibility, transforms and " deforms " infinitely. This deification is better received, assuredly, in the Adamic purity of God's image restored in the " place of the heart " — which allows monotheistic mysticism to integrate the spiritual dimension of the East. But this transformation is nevertheless received or infused, and not regained or reconquered (as in neo-Platonizing Sufism) — by which Moslem faith and mysticism, whose connection to the pre-Islamic spirituality of the Desert Fathers is likely, exhibit in Eastern lands a major element of Christian orthodoxy.

Beyond the political borders of Christendom, and on the eve of the schism between the Eastern and Western Churches, Hallâjian contemplation continues the mysticism of the early Christian anchorites and paves the way for the mysticism of Saint John of the Cross. Already with Al-Hallâj, interiorization has ceased to be a mere efficacious technique, and has become purgative humility. In the opinion of Miguel Asín Palacios, Saint John of the Cross received from Ibn Abbâd of Ronda, last of the great Andalusian Sufis, the idea of " dark night; " but — assuming the accuracy of this hypothesis — he not only made this image his own, he also incorporated it into the mystery of the Trinity, which is unknown to Islam. To him, the same Holy Spirit who is " the deepest center of the soul, " is also the one " who draws out the soul from every creature and from itself. "

Branch of the Christian tree which in Al-Hallâj recovered the memory of its roots, spiritual bridge between East and West, Moslem mysticism found in Spanish soil its providential conclusion. The history of the dialogue between God and those who seek Him is indeed mysterious but coherent.

[1] Regarding interiority in the Brahmanic (or intellectual) phase of Hindu tradition, from the twin viewpoint of the involution of cosmic consciousness (by virtue of the " constitutive correlation " between microcosm and macrocosm) and the reabsorption of the ego in the impersonal *Brahma,* refer to Olivier Lacombe : " Le Védânta comme Méthode de Spiritualité " (*Revue Thomiste,* I-III, 1956, p. 88 ff.). In one form or another, the same tendency appears in all non-Monotheistic spiritualities, and even in the Jewish and Islamic schools of mysticism. Cf., at the end of the analysis quoted above, the typical example of the " diver " sinking before he reaches the spot where the " I am " rises from the water. This example is taken from the *Ullada Narpadu,* or " Knowledge of Being, " by Shrî Ramana Maharshi, the great Hindu contemplative who died in 1950. His uninterrupted state of complete interiorization started suddenly in 1895, when he was seventeen, with the spontaneous " experience " of his own death and self-survival. He continuously " contemplated all things as being within himself, " in the words used by Shankara to describe the state of a *yogi (Atma-Bodha).*

[2] " Expériences mystiques en terres non-chrétiennes " (p. 85), in *Sagesse et Cultures* (a series under the editorship of Jacques Maritain), Paris 1953.

[3] It seems to us that the common denominator, the fundamental structure of all religions is the awareness of the Sacred, i. e., the consciousness of the " Completely Other " as *mysterium tremendum et fascinans,* according to the definition of Rudolf Otto. But we would gain only a superficial view of things if we were to take this general structure for the innermost core of each religion, and thus to confuse their common base with their common summit. The difference between a yogi and a saint — the respective summits of Hinduism and Christianity — is much greater than between a devout Shivaite and a devout Christian. And precisely in this irreducible difference appears the " specific " essence, the individual and ultimate features of the two religions in question.

[4] *Atmâ,* literally the reflexive pronoun, is translated as " the Self, " with a capital, to emphasize its suprasubjective and transpsychological essence.

[5] *Loc. cit.,* p. 14.

[6] Sir John Woodroffe, a British judge in India who is the leading translator of Tantric writings, and the noted sinologist Albert de Pouvourville both returned to Catholicism. The Sanskrit scholar and Protestant theologian Rudolf Otto, author of the well known treatise entitled *The Sacred,* is indebted to Hindu mysticism for having deepened his

faith and gained awareness of the value of liturgy. It hardly seems necessary to recall how much Father de Foucauld owed to his acquaintance with Moslem mysticism, which is so typical of the culmination of interiority in monotheistic transcendency. We will also mention the significant title of the autobiographical account by Father Wallace, S.J., an English missionary : *From Evangelism to Catholicism by way of India.* Finally, there is the case of Julian Green, whose conversion from total unbelief to Christian fervor began with a Buddhist phase.

[7] " Toward an absolute which bursts the framework of time, man has at his disposal only an initial movement of interiorization, a first retorsion of self upon self, " writes Louis Gardet, *op. cit.*, p. 13.

[8] To appreciate this complementary nature fully, one should recall the Patristic formula according to which " the world was created of the Father, by the Son, and in the Holy Spirit. "

There are many variations of the saying quoted in the text above. Saint Augustine expressed it as follows : " Thou wast even more inward than my innermost self, and higher than the uppermost summit of my being " (*Tu autem eras inferior intimo meo et superior summo meo, Conf.*, III, VI, 11).

[9] On the surpassing of oneself from within, refer to Saint Augustine, *Enarr. in Psalmos* 38, 1-3; 41, 8; 61, 14; and particularly 76, 9 ff. The ascent toward God begins, he writes, when we leave ourselves behind : " Then there is no more danger, for the danger lies in remaining within ourselves. "

[10] Derived from " Gentile, " i. e., non-Jew. Today, one prefers to avoid the overly scornful term of " pagan. "

At the end of his remarkable study entitled *God in Patristic Thought*, the late G. L. Prestige, Canon of St. Paul's Cathedral, notes that the principles of transcendency, creation, and immanence, in their relationship to the universe, respectively typify the Father (" Origin without origin "), the Son (redeemer or re-creator), and the Holy Spirit (regulator of the world *ab intra* and sanctifier of man). According to the Greek Fathers, however, man's ascent toward God takes place in the opposite direction or order, from the Holy Spirit — who " is more inward to us than ourselves " —, through the Son — " image of the Father, " just as the Spirit is " the image of the Son " —, *toward the Father.* Cf., for instance, Saint John Damascene, *De fide orth.* I, 13, and Saint Irenaeus, *loc. cit.* The same ascending ternary progression marks the three parts of the Mass of the Faithful. None can pass from the interiority of the Holy Spirit to the " Abyss of the Father, " save " through the Son. " The Spirit brings man back to his inner center, to his ontological core, not for man to sink within himself, but so that,

in his center, he may find himself as image of God open to the absolute
transcendency, i. e., as a person capable of surrendering freely and entirely
to the dominion of crucified Love (Offertory), a Love which consumes
and recreates the person, assimilating it to Christ (Consecration), through,
with and in Whom the Father returns the person, transformed into a son
of God, to itself and to the world (Communion). Assumed by the Holy
Spirit — Whom Saint Basil calls " intellectual Light " —, " Eastern "
contemplation is clearly continued and fulfilled in the trinitarian mystery
of God hidden and revealed in His very incarnation.

[11] Fr. Taymans d'Eypernon, S.J. : *Les paradoxes du Bouhddisme*,
p. XI. Among the ruins of the Church of *la Merced de Cuzco* may be seen
this beautiful inscription : " We must find Christ in the soul of the native. "

[12] We have already referred (page 33, Footnote 5) to Father
Teilhard de Chardin's hypothesis of a human-and-cosmic Consciousness
converging both toward itself and toward Christ-Omega, of a universe
focusing, from its inception, " toward states of higher and higher
interiorization, and of increasingly complete reflection " (*Apparition de
l'Homme*, p. 367, Editions du Seuil 1956), but a universe in which, on the
other hand, " all the conscious gathers within itself all the individual
consciousnesses . . ., each one becoming more itself, and thus more distinct,
as it draws closer to the conscious in Omega " (*Le Phénomène humain*, p. 291);
" a universe which, therefore, is ultimately lovable and loving " (*App.
de l'Homme*, p. 373). In a sense, this constitutes a transformist cosmogenesis,
but one in which, contrary to the opinion of the determinists and the
metaphysicians who are influenced by them, universality is the opposite
of impersonality, and mystery is the opposite of anonymity.

At the root of this conception, might there not be a fundamentally
contemplative intuition of the fact that interiority " begets " the person
by culminating in transcendency, an intuition which this paleontologist-
priest, who explored much of Asia, translated into modern scientific
language? His " Biosphere " and " Noosphere " are strongly reminiscent
of the " Soul of the World " and the " World of the *Noûs* " of Plotinus,
whose ideas in turn resemble and may possibly be related to Hindu
contemplation, which aims at integrating the universe through " involution "
of cosmic consciousness. Perhaps Father Teilhard de Chardin's work
has created such wide interest because, basically, it constitutes a cosmo-
mystical " state " which is " interpreted " by projection on the screen
of scientific facts, because it has been successful in summoning and verifying
*ab extra*, in objective terms of observation and experience, the *ab intra*
vision of " Universal Man, " the inner experience of the Beauty of the

World in God. A nostalgia for this Beauty, frustrated up to now by modern science, lies deep within every soul.

This striking coincidence has not received all the attention it deserves : it is exactly since the discovery of heliocentrism that, paradoxically enough, Western civilization has become individualistic and antipersonalistic, and therefore spiritually egocentric. Facing in the opposite direction from materialistic and deterministic evolutionism, Father Teilhard de Chardin's Christocentric evolutionism actually does no more than restore to Copernican heliocentrism its true spiritual meaning, and has thus shown that, if the universe of modern science appeared to turn away from revealed faith, " scientism " and not science is to blame. From the viewpoint of the Meeting of the two religious hemispheres, it seems highly significant that this eminent naturalist achieved such a result by " incorporating " into the Christian faith an eminently " Oriental " dimension.

[13] " Considered in its state of separation from the body, the human soul, as we (the Christians) know it, will very nearly coincide with the (Buddhist) concept of the person who has entered Nirvâna " (Fr. Taymans d'Eypernon, S.J., *op. cit.*, p. 213). In this context, see pp. 58 below and 46 above.

In the book which he has just devoted to Amidism, and which had not yet come to our attention when these lines were written (*Amida*, Editions du Seuil, 1955), Father Henri de Lubac wonders whether, " for this (Buddhist) soul and for those like it, perhaps for a multitude whose spiritual life has left no trace, . . . Amida did not actually constitute one of the names, one of the pseudonymous apparitions, or at least the distant substitute, of the one God, the only Saviour . . . " (p. 306).

A Tibetan lama pointed out to a Christian missionary that, if mankind applied the principles of the Buddha, the world would live in peace. " And if it practiced the doctrines of Christ, " asked the missionary, " what would be the result? " " It would assuredly be heaven on earth, " answered the lama. " Why then do you not become a convert to Christianity? ", insisted the other. " Because you, the Westerners, do not live by it, " replied the Buddhist.

On the " Buddhism of Faith ", see in particular E. Conze : *Buddhism*, The Philosophical Library, New York, pp. 144 and 55.

[14] The doctrinal antagonism between these two pinnacles of Hindu spirituality forms the subject of the classical treatise by Olivier Lacombe : *L'Absolu selon le Védânta*.

The equation *âtmâ = Brahma* designates the fundamental identity existing between the divine Absolute and our true Self, considered as both prior and superior to all our ordinary empirical " egos, " be they corporeal (" I am tall, " " I am hungry ") or incorporeal (" I desire, " " I want, " " I love, " " I think "). Its classical formulation is the *Tat tvam asi* (*id tu es :* thou art That), which the master repeats to his disciple in connection with the unperceivable essence underlying all things or any " object " and, finally, in relation to the Supreme Brahma " who is the most subtle of the subtle, who is eternal, who is none other than yourself " *(Kaivalya Upanishad)*.

¹⁵ Olivier Lacombe, *Râmânuja*, in " Approches de l'Inde, " *Les Cahiers du Sud*, 1949, p. 122.

¹⁶ In order to emphasize this paradox, we will recall that Hindus, since the Trinity of Persons within the Divinity is unknown to them, cannot imagine that extreme unity is compatible with full distinction and, consequently, with complete freedom in the sense of voluntary and reciprocal interpersonal communication. For a Hindu, spiritual liberty means fullness of being, fulfilled possession, and not surrender to the Other.

In the opinion of J. Monchanin, a missionary who is now living as an ascetic among Hindu ascetics, only the Mystery of the Trinity is capable of resolving the antinomies which cause Hindu thought to swing endlessly between monism and pluralism, between a personal and an impersonal God. India, he writes, " awaits without knowing it the Revelation of the Trinitarian Mystery, a Revelation inaccessible both to metaphysical genius and to holiness " *(Dieu Vivant*, 1945, No. 3).

Since intersubjectivity *in divinis* is unknown to Hindu Trinitarian speculation, we will specify, in terms of Christian theology, that this speculation oscillates between the heresy of " Modalism " and that of " Tritheism. " Indeed, it would be Modalism to reduce the three divine Persons to three " aspects " of God, such as *Sachchidânanda* (" Being-Knowledge-Beatitude "), and Tritheism to see in Them the three gods of the *Trimurti* (Brahma-Vishnu-Shiva, in their immanent functions of production, conservation, and reabsorption or " transformation ").

¹⁷ Here are a few verses of this invocation : " Like Jesus on the gibbet of love, I repeat my profession of love. Like Jesus, I am the fixed point of everything, manifest or hidden. Like Jesus in the maternal womb, I have opened a way between being and nothingness. I have reached the essence of Jesus. Like Jesus on the gibbet, I have been transmuted into Certitude. "

¹⁸ " The posthumous survival of Al-Hallâj in Islam, " writes his Catholic biographer Louis Massignon, " bears ample witness to the fact

that, in a positive way, crucified Love is life and resurrection " (*Dieu Vivant*, No. 4, p. 37).

[19] " The first step toward unification in God *(tawhîd)* is the complete suppression of isolation *(tajrîd)*, " declares Al-Hallâj. At this point, we will recall that, for Origen, it was " spiritual satiety " which caused the fall of the angels. According to the Koran's version — which is Christian in origin — of Adam's creation, *Iblis* (Lucifer) fell because he considered it unworthy of his luminous nature to bow before the first man, as Allah had ordered the angels to do. Al-Hallâj sees in Iblis the first " monist, " because he was unwilling to adore anything outside the one God : in other words, Iblis accepted to adore God only in so far as He disregards His creature.

# 6

# Equalitarian
# Correspondence
# or Spiritual Charity?


The preceding pages suggest the following conclusion : all religions do indeed converge toward the one universal God. But it does not necessarily follow that all religions are more or less equivalent, as asserted (in agreement with Radhakrishnan) by many fervent Western admirers of the Orient. Nor does it follow that there can only exist differences of degree between them, as believed by past and present traditionalists on the one hand, and by rationalistic or idealistic evolutionists on the other. To a Christian student of history, the spiritual evolution of mankind is neither a stage in a perpetual cyclic pattern, nor a result of purely human aspirations, nor again the history of God gradually becoming aware of Himself (as maintained by Hegel). Instead, it is the history of the concrete and reciprocal relationship between the image of God in man, obscured by original sin, and the Creator of the universe, a history made of human refusals and divine silences, of imperfect appeals and freely given answers.

## Qualitative Aspect of Religious Time.

All men in all times have been created in the image of God, and hence *for* God — which is enough to explain the convergence of religions. But an image is not a resemblance, deiformity *in posse* is not deiformity *in esse*. No man, by his own devices, has ever bridged the distance from one to the other, a distance equal to the immeasurable interval between nature and Grace, which became an abyss as a result of original sin. Is it not to the effect of this congenital, inveterate and universal sin of pride that we should attribute the illusion, so widespread in the Orient, that man by himself is capable of bringing out, restoring or developing his original deiformity? Can we properly ascribe to any other source the unjustified conviction of being able inwardly to regain the lost paradise, by means of a contemplative technique at once unfailing and subject to our will? And if such be the results of original sin, is it not in the final analysis to the divine Condescension, to the gratuitous overtures of the offended Love, that one must assign the fact that the spiritual History of the East constitutes a gradual lifting of this illusion? Hindu historians themselves divide the evolution of India into three phases : a ritual period (*karma-marga*, until about 1000 B.C.), an intellectual period (*inâna-marga*, from 1000 B.C. to approximately the dawn of the Christian era), and finally a period during which spiritual love predominates (*bhakti-marga*, from the beginning of the Christian era — time of the *Bhagavad-Gita* — to the present day) [1]. The Christian outlook allows us to see in the increasingly " monotheistic " orientation of these three phases a " divine economy, " a transhistorical Plan in relation to which the spiritual evolution of mankind, ordered to the " eighth day of creation, " is neither more nor less than an immense prelude to the Parousia [2]. When Pascal declares that everything remains incomprehensible without the incomprehensible mystery of the fall and of redemption, he expresses a truth which is applicable on the scale of universal history. The Fathers of the Church, when they included the entire known *orbis terrarum* in their inspired Christocentric vision, left us with the task of embracing the global horizon of the modern world in the same vision. Outside this perspective, the inevitable and disturbing problem of non-Christian religions places us in danger of falling into one of the following extremes : Pharisaic exclusivism, which sins against spiritual charity, and destructive tolerantism, which is guilty of " confusionism. " The former betrays Love, and the latter betrays Christ.

Here are some examples of the second extreme :

*Incarnation and Avatâra.*

Most European and American works devoted to Hindu doctrines translate by " incarnation " the word *avatâra*, which actually denotes the " descents, " " earthly manifestations, " or " theophanies " of the compassionate Vishnu. Only one step more is required to consider Christ as an *avatâra*, intended for the West, of the same god, and this step is unhesitatingly taken by several Orientalists and all occultists. They base their " concordism " on the fact that *Krishna*, the last human appearance of the god Vishnu, promised supreme deliverance to any man who " abandons the fruit of his deeds " and denies himself " for love of Me " *(Bhagavad-Gita)*. There is no need to invoke the animal manifestations of Vishnu, nor even to discuss the historicity of this human theophany, in order to realize at once that Hindus do not in the least believe that their God, in appearing to Arjuna under the human features of his comrade-in-arms Krishna, really assumed our weak nature, including a human body, or actually suffered as a truly incarnate man. For Hindus, Vishnu merely took on the appearance of a human being; beyond this appearance, he never ceased to remain pure god, unaffected by our vicissitudes. A Christian who calls this event " incarnation " strays, perhaps unconsciously, into the heresy of " Docetism " (derived from *dokeô* = to appear), which teaches that the humanity of Christ is only apparent. Hindus are " Docetists " by temperament and tradition, and it is difficult for them to concede that God's Love for men is more than a condescension. The fact that divinity as such can actually, in the words of Saint Paul, " empty itself " of its majesty, is beyond them. They consider it contradictory that God be humbled and crucified without ceasing to be God and, for them, contradictory is synonymous with impossible, never with " supernatural paradox [3]. "

We are tempted to say that the radiant figure of Krishna represents what the " incarnation " *would have been* if it had followed logic, if the divine answer to the mystical aspirations of man were predictable. The disconcerting figure of the Crucified Christ reveals what the incarnation *is* when God makes it a reality. This is why Christian love — *agapê* — possesses unsuspected features which distinguish it from Hindu *bhakti*, and also from Platonic *erôs*. The worshipper of Krishna, for example, feels " capable of God " *because* and to the extent that he is worthy of Him, whereas in the presence of Christ man finds himself *capax Dei although* he is unworthy of Him. A Christian knows that God does not love him for his own worth, but on the contrary that he has worth because God loves him. Therefore, *agapê* can not be reduced to *bhakti* or *erôs*, as the modernists believe, but neither does it exclude them, as the Puritans would have it [4]. *Agapê* gathers, reorients and transfigures these non-Christian forms of love, without abolishing or absorbing them. It rises on them like the sun on a faintly lit city, altering nothing but enhancing every detail.

### Buddhist Love (Maitrî) and Christian Charity (Agapê).

In Greece as in India, spiritual love is never directed toward one's neighbor. *Erôs* rises from man to the divine, and *bhakti*, in addition, descends from God to man, but in both cases the " others " (the worshipper's fellow creatures) appear to be excluded, as it were, from the spiritual circuit. In the sermons of the Buddha (sixth Century B.C.), on the other hand, we find, for the first time in non-Biblical spirituality, exhortations such as these : " All the religious acts of our life, O Monks, are worth but the sixteenth part of the love of living beings *(maitrî) ;* this love, which frees the spirit, gathers the

other deeds within itself; it shines, sparkles and glows [5]. "
" As a mother gives even her life to protect her child, her only
son, so should be (in a monk) the unlimited benevolence toward
all other beings; he should be animated by an inexhaustible
love for the whole world [6]. " Many authors wonder whether
this is not the purest form of Christian charity; something
even purer than evangelical charity, add a few writers, since
*maitrî* extends, beyond men, to all creatures. " Caritative breadth
unknown to the West before Saint Francis of Assisi, "
triumphantly exclaim those who harbor feelings of resentment
against Christian civilization; and they quote the initiation
vow of the *bodhisattvas* (or " future buddhas ") " not to enter
*nirvâna* before the last blade of grass is also released from
suffering. " Entranced with universalism, they overlook this
elementary truth : " Grasp all, lose all. "

Love of neighbor can have as object either the mortal
individuality or the spiritual person of our fellow creature.
If the study of Buddhist scriptures leads us to the conclusion
that, in either case, an abyss separates the Buddhist and the
Christian conceptions of " neighbor, " then we will have to
decide that Charity and *maitrî* cannot be identical.

In the first case, when the object of love is one's neighbor
as an individual, the divergence is complete. According to
Buddhist doctrine, the neighbor's individuality is devoid of
reality, not only in relation to God — who is unknown to
Buddhism as a distinct and subsistent Being —, but also in
relation to his fellow men. It is not merely correct, but eminently
salutary as well, to see in every individuality nothing more
than a suffering psychophysical conglomerate, momentarily
" united " by the binding force of the congenital " craving to
exist. " The mistake of equating these two forms of love arises
from the fact that both Christian *agapê* and Buddhist *maitrî*
consist in loving one's neighbor as oneself. But whereas the
former connects two equally real individualities, both created

in the " image of God, " the latter occurs between two equally
" suffering, impermanent and unsubstantial aggregates, " in
the words of the time honored formula. " Since it is not taken
seriously ", the individuality of our fellow man " can not be
the object of a serious love [7]. " *Maitrî* is not charity, but only
commiseration. A Buddhist must love the individuality of his
neighbor as little as his own, which is why *maitrî* can and must
extend equally to men, animals and plants. Charity, on the other
hand, is more than compassion; it implies no imperfection
in the neighbor, it loves him as a fellow creature and as much
as self, which is why it can and must be concentrated on man.
Buddhist love loses in intensity what it gains in breadth [8].

If we now consider our neighbor as a spiritual person,
another difference appears between *agapê* and *maitrî*. The former,
charitable love — including love of neighbor —, is an *end* in
itself, because its object (the human person) is the " image
and likeness " of a God who is Love itself [9]. *Maitrî* or
compassionate love, on the other hand, is a means subordinate
to an end other than love, namely *nirvâna* (literally " despi-
ration "). Indeed, this final state is regarded as being beyond
love, since it implies that consciousness of both one's own
and the neighbor's separate individuality is uprooted and
destroyed, and therefore also consciousness of our fellow
man's spiritual person as " other. " Buddhism is not unaware
of the person, as has been so often maintained, but it considers
the person from a purely dynamic viewpoint which is the opposite
of the Christian outlook [10]. Like Hinduism, Buddhism sees
the human person as disincarnate, completely divorced from
individuality; in addition, however, Buddhism defines the
person as something which is " to be born, " and which " is
made " only to the extent that the ego " is unmade ", as a pure
act of " entering *nirvâna* ", pure " awakening [11]. " In other
words, the Buddhist person, at the moment when it is born,
already coincides with that of other " awakened ones. "
According to Buddhism, the neighbor's person must merge

or fuse with " mine " before it can become the object of a spiritual
act; the " other " can not reach the dignity of spiritual person
as long as he remains distinct from " me. " This is why Buddhist
love, at the very moment when it could become caritative,
turns into self-love, " falls back " into love of the universal
" Self " *(âtmâ)* : " I have traveled throughout the world without
finding anything which one might love more than one's Self [12]. "
Far from growing outward toward the neighbor, *maitrî* is
neutralized in him : " He who has a hundred kinds of love
has a hundred kinds of suffering..., he who has one love
has one suffering, he who has no love has no suffering, " preached
the Buddha. He held that solidarity with the neighbor's suffering
consists essentially in " interchanging one's own ego with
that of others; " this solidarity is an ideal " raft " on which
to cross the bitter stream of existence, but (he added) one does
not carry a raft on one's shoulders once the other bank is reached.
Gautama Buddha aspired, not to reach consummation in
disinterested fervor, but to be consumed in impassive serenity
*(upekkhâ)*. He embraced all living creatures so that he might
everywhere embrace himself under the guise of his neighbor [13].

### *Error and Sin; Illusion and Disobedience.*

Buddhism, and in general all the spiritual East — with
the notable exception of Islam — consider the ego as a fundamental illusion. " Good " therefore, in this perspective, does
not consist in purifying the individuality, but in uprooting it.
For the same reason, " evil " is not, in the eyes of the East,
the concrete result of a free disobedience, but only the illusory
reflection of a fatal subjectivism, and coincides with individuation
as such. So understood, " evil " can not possibly be considered
as stemming from an original and hereditary sin which it
behooves us to atone for; it can only be seen as the inevitable
consequence of an immemorial and inveterate error. Our task,
a task both necessary and sufficient, is to dispel this error

by becoming aware of our true nature, which has remained
innocent and unpolluted. The nonmonotheistic East is unaware
of sin; it has no conception, therefore, of the purgative virtue
of repentance, of its humiliating demands, power of recon-
ciliation, or " caritative " dimension. Beguiled by the unhoped
for existence of a " spirituality without sin, " several Western
writers have thought that the doctrine of original sin might
merely express, with the help of a purely symbolic episode,
this immemorial and inevitable " fall into individuation [14]. "
Fault and sin would thus be reduced, in the final analysis, to
a simple " error in perspective. " Just the opposite is true.
The Maker of the universe paradoxically manifesting Himself
as Father, and above all the effulgent presence of Christ
" agonizing even to the end of time, " have revealed hitherto
unsuspected dimensions of freedom and mercy; these are
" divine events " which overthrow and correct our views,
revelations capable (when experienced inwardly) of making
us recognize and feel as original fault, inexcusable yet redeemed,
that which could appear, without these events, as mere congenital
ignorance, an ignorance we would be free to either perpetuate
or overcome. At the root of our confusion, sufferings and
anguish, we can and must now recognize, not a fateful
misapprehension arising from a gradual surrender to a collective
illusion, but a lie, a deliberate subversion, for which the unity
of mankind makes us coresponsible; a willful refusal of Love,
a hateful ingratitude, a mortal stain, of which each of my sins
shows me to be an accomplice. We can no longer blame
a progressive and immemorial " sinking " of mankind, a mere
contagious delusion, from which I would be free to break
away and " save myself for me alone. " Knowing as we do
at what price we have been redeemed, a reduction of evil to
a fateful mirage superimposed over a blissful and impassive
Reality would imply on our part a refusal to behold the Passion,
so as to avoid seeing ourselves, as in a mirror, capable of
wounding God to the point of shedding His blood.

### Comments Concerning Ramakrishna.

Fascinated by the teachings and the figure of Christ, Ramakrishna forsook the Hindu rites for a time (in 1885), to become absorbed in Jesus Christ, to the point where he seemed to be changed into a Christian mystic. " He traveled the road of Christianity, " proclaimed his biographers, his disciples, and his Hindu and European admirers, " he experienced its authenticity, thus demonstrating that Christianity is a way which also leads to perfect absorption in the divine Consciousness. " We believe that the truth of the matter is more complex. Was it really the Christian road which the " Saint of Dakshineshwar " traveled in striving to imitate Christ? Was it not rather, once again, the way of his own native *bhakti-yoga*, but with the inspiration of the Gospels, just as he had previously drawn inspiration from Islamic mysticism? Upon examining this period of his life more closely, one soon realizes that Christianity, in fact, was for him only an opportunity to repeat the experience of his countless mystical raptures *(samâdhis)*. For instance, it was enough for him to contemplate for the first time, at the house of a friend, a picture of the Virgin and Child, in order to lose consciousness and " enter into *samâdhi*, " although Christianity was still unknown to him. Then, after he had meditated for three days on the life of Jesus, a human figure appeared to him and he heard an inner voice which called upon this vision, addressing it as " Redeemer, " " Incarnate Love " and " Master Yogi; " he saw the figure draw nearer and — this detail is highly significant — gradually become part of him. What this remarkable experience " demonstrated " is not the truth of Christianity, but only Shri Ramakrishna's exceptional spiritual plasticity. His case is actually the reverse of Al-Hallâj's, which has already been mentioned : far from being " grafted onto Christ, " Ramakrishna incorporated into the Hindu perspective those elements of Christianity which he had assimilated. Had he really " experienced its truth, "

as asserted by his disciples, he (who was so communicative)
would surely have told his familiars something about the
Christian mysteries; he would at least have caught a glimpse
of the nature — not only undifferentiated, but also tripersonal —
of the divine Unity. In actual fact, nothing allows us to assume
that he ever imagined the possibility of an intradivine Love,
from infinite Person to infinite Person, nor that he ever ceased
confusing Incarnation with *Avatâra*. When his Hindu biographer
declares that Ramakrishna " realized his identity with Christ,
as he had realized it with Kâli, Râma, Hanumân, Krishna,
Brahma and Mohammed, " it becomes clear how much the
Oriental tendency to " unite in order to dissolve " calls for
a corrective, if the dialogue between religions is not to
degenerate into a monologue. And whoever is not blinded
by anti-Western bias will recognize that this corrective actually
exists, and is to be found in the complementary tendency to
" separate in order to unite, " which distinguishes Western
spirituality.

This is indeed a " providential " contrast, for these
two tendencies are contrary without being contradictory :
they are antinomic. A discussion of antinomic knowledge will
form the subject of our conclusion.

* * *

[1] On this subject, see : Louis Renou, *L'Inde Classique* (Payot);
H. von Glasenapp, *Les Philosophies de l'Inde* (French translation from the
German, published by Maisonneuve); and Olivier Lacombe, " Le Védânta
comme Méthode de Spiritualité " (*Revue Thomiste*, I-III, 1956, pp. 89 and
97 ff.)

[2] When man takes one step toward God, say the Sufis, He rises
from His throne and takes a hundred steps toward man. — Perhaps we
should say " reorientation " rather than " orientation, " for the oldest
Vedic writings are more " monotheistic " than " metaphysical " in outlook.
Witness, among many other indications, the name Dyauspiter — the Greek
Zeus-Pater — of the most ancient God of the sky. Regarding the funda-

mentally personal conception of God among the most primitive and isolated peoples, see the *Manuel d'Histoire comparée des Religions*, by the ethnologist P. W. Schmidt, Chapter XVII. He points out that the tribes which have retained their original characteristics practice monotheism, monogamy and pacifism.

We see in this an indication of the fact that the original Fall obscured, but did not destroy, the memory of primal Revelation, and that the " progress " of civilization has often dimmed this remembrance still further.

³ Even the Koran, although eminently monotheistic, refuses on this point to accept the paradox of the mystery, and resolves it by maintaining that Christ was not actually crucified : " They neither killed nor crucified Him, but His double was substituted before their eyes . . ., they did not really kill Him, but on the contrary Allah raised Him toward Himself " (Surate IV, 156-158).

⁴ According to Nygren, *Erôs* and *Agapê* (this is the title of his famous book, published by Aubier) are incompatible because the former — the impulse toward eternal Beauty — consists in an ascending and " egocentric " movement, while the latter — freely given and caritative love — is a pure descent of God toward the creature and, through the creature, toward the neighbor. If these two terms were indeed incompatible, how could one explain that Gregory of Nyssa calls *erôs* the ecstatic height of *agapê*, and that mystical *erôs*, for Dionysius the Areopagite, can and should end and reach full development in love of one's neighbor (a facet of *agapê* unknown to the Greeks and Hindus)? Nygren's anticontemplative inclination leads him to confuse " interiority " with " egocentrism, " which prevents him from recognizing that the two " movements " are at bottom complementary, and that the Platonic *erôs* (" natural mysticism "), incorporated into Christian spirituality, can and should culminate in an aspiration capable of " going *forth* to meet " Grace. If *erôs* and *agapê* were mutually exclusive, *bhakti* (which at the start coincides with Platonic *erôs*) could not have reached the intuition of Grace, as we have indicated; it would have received no " divine answer. "

⁵ *Itivuttaka*, 27.

⁶ *Suttanipata*, 149.

⁷ Henri de Lubac, *Aspects du Bouddhisme*, p. 36.

⁸ The example of Saint Francis of Assisi, whom Dante called " sun of the East, " amply demonstrates that charity also embraces compassion for all creatures. Instead of reducing caritative love to compassion, however, Christianity subordinates the latter to the former. Christian compassion

is integrated and " centered, " so to speak, in love of man, because man is the epitome and the conclusion of the entire creation, and because he is therefore, as Saint Paul points out, responsible for the spiritual destiny of all living creatures (*Rom.* 8 : 21). The study of Buddhist love, of its nobility and limitations, throws into full relief the paradoxical and seemingly inordinate assertion of Saint Paul : " If I should deliver my body to be burned, and have not charity, it profiteth me nothing " (I *Cor.* 13 : 3).

[9] According to the Greek Fathers, " resemblance, " as we have shown, expresses the consummation or actualization of the potential deiformity of the " image. " This gradation corresponds with the culmination of the " psychic body " in the " spiritual body " (to quote Saint Paul), i. e., of egocentric individuality in theocentric personality. " The soul can have as perfect a habitus of charity in this life as in the other " (Saint John of the Cross, *Flame*, I, 14).

[10] *Actus sequitur esse*, " action follows being, " typifies the Aristotelian and Thomistic West, just as perfectly as the opposite formulation, *esse sequitur actum*, " being follows action, " or " we are what we do, " could define the logic of the entire Buddhist Orient.

[11] The universe, say the Buddhists, is a sowing of men, and mankind a sowing of Buddhas.

[12] *Udâna*, V, 1.

[13] Over against love of " neighbor, " it will be remembered that Nietzsche extolled love of " the far away " *(Fernstenliebe)*.

[14] Professed from the dawn of the Christian era by the Gnostic heterodoxy, then by the Manicheans, revived during the Middle Ages by the Bogomiles and the Catharians, this outlook was tirelessly opposed by the Church.

# CONCLUSION

## *Antinomic Knowledge, the Opening of Intelligence to Mystery.*

In accordance with Patristic tradition, we call " antinomy " an opposition, the terms of which remain incompatible in the natural order and reveal themselves as complementary only in the supernatural order [1]. It is truly a compound or second-degree paradox. To qualify as an antinomy, it is not enough that a paradox be insoluble by discursive reasoning, for this would not lead us out of the natural order. It must also be without issue for our intellectual intuition. And an antinomic paradox is without issue, not because it is insoluble absolutely, but because divine revelation is its only focus of resolution. Its spiritual function is precisely this tension, which directs the entire being, including supra-rational intelligence, beyond itself. This tension, by closing every intelligible issue other than God, allows the mind to find in Him alone the " coincidence of opposites; " it lifts up and focuses the mind in this " place of God, " to use the words of Evagrius Ponticus, where the mind becomes receptive only to an increate Answer. Carrying the " thirst for God " to the very heights of consciousness, the antinomic movement draws along intelligence itself into humble love, into the " ineffable groaning " of the Spirit.

The Meeting of Religions has brought to light new antinomies, and has revived one of the deepest : that of interiority and transcendency. For these antinomies to be fruitful, it is essential to distinguish without separating, so as to unite without confusing.

This ability is a legacy of the hypostatic union. When mingled, two separate bodies cease to be distinct; body and soul, however, although more intimately united than any mixture, nevertheless remain perfectly distinct. " Without confusion or transformation, " but also " without separation or division, " divine nature and human nature both constitute " the same Christ, " proclaimed the Council of Chalcedon fifteen hundred years ago. It is in this same " union which does not eliminate distinction " that our human person, indivisibly body and soul, communes through Grace with the Person of Him Who will be " all in all. " As soon as the will to unite weakens, the Western capacity for differentiation becomes a propensity to separate or isolate, and degenerates into fanaticism; the Eastern ability for unification, on the other hand, if it seeks to merge that which is distinct to the extent of denying God when He reveals Himself as Other than pure anonymous indistinction, withdraws from Grace and degenerates (particularly as imitated in the West) into syncretism and tolerantism. Hypostatic union is the narrow path between these two extremes.

A fanatic is not one who considers that some particular tenet of Eastern religions is incompatible with the Christian dogma, an obvious fact on the level of human formulations; instead, a fanatic is a person unwilling to ask himself what really takes place between God and the soul of the Oriental who, after the most disinterested ascetic efforts, reaches what he calls *nirvâna, samâdhi* or *tawhîd;* it is a man incapable of associating in his mind such distant fellow creatures with the divine Infinity, probably because it is not in God that he loves those closer to him either. We witness here a meeting of the two extremes.

Tolerantism, indeed, does not consist in loving all men in God, but in loving only the human values. It is a despiritualized love, secularized through insensitivity to or resentment against supernatural values. The very word tolerance seems unsuitable to us in matters of comparative religion, at least in so far as the term suggests a certain disdain for that which is "tolerated," a condescension which so often conceals, beneath apparent sympathy, a deep indifference to religion as such. We are not faced with a problem of tolerance, but of understanding; in the final analysis, it is a question of integrating the various antinomies through the transfiguring vision and power of incarnate Love. Christ and Saint Paul did not come in order to tolerate, nor even to teach (may we add with Pascal), but to set afire.

In an atmosphere of mere tolerance, the parable of the blind men and the elephant, which we mentioned earlier, would be conclusive, and the "terrible simplifiers" would be right. When placed in a perspective of antinomic understanding, however, this illustration is seen to be wanting. Even if one is willing, for the sake of allegory, to liken the Unfathomable Divine Reality to an elephant, and the various religions to as many blind men attempting to guess the shape of the beast, we will point out that each blind man does not approach the truth to the same degree; he who touches the head discovers something more than his companions who call "elephant" the animal's back or legs. This is because the body of a living being — and all the more so mankind in its relationship to God — constitutes a whole which is more significant than the sum of its constituent parts, a hierarchic entity whose elements are never equivalent or interchangeable. The fallacy of this parable is that it reduces the various religions to mere "viewpoints" (symbolized by tactile sensations lacking visual confirmation), i. e., to purely subjective outlooks unsupported by objectively available data, which is a postulate common to all forms of idealism. Actually, the reality which confronts the subject — whether this reality be of a religious nature or of any other nature — is, to all practical purposes, always prior to the subject, at the very least contemporary with and never posterior to him; the subject does not "posit" reality, he finds it. The parable assumes that God is "given" only as an Essence incapable of being translated into objective terms, an Essence prior to the distinction between subject and object; the parable excludes the possibility that God might objectively "give Himself." In fact, whether we consider the manifestations of the impersonal and transobjective Deity, or the revelations of the transcendent Person of God, religious forms and ways also precede the subject; they are objective values, and values imply an ordered hierarchy. It is not man's role to "posit" them as being all equivalent, but to receive them as they are. If the elephant is replaced by a human figure, the difference which we have pointed out between the head and the body appears even more clearly as a qualitative difference, a difference of value which the subject receives and discovers, on the border between nature and Grace. We do not think it improper to imagine that this human figure felt in the night be that of the God-Man who has opened so many blind eyes to the Face of the Unbegotten Father. This leads us out of the field of parable or evocative symbolism, and into the realm of the truly infinite and infinitely "given" transparency of incarnate Grace, to that supernatural light which the Magi, on a winter night nearly two thousand years ago, were among the very first to behold.

### Knowledge of Faith.

To say, as we have done several times, that Christ is "The Face of the Father," is to express in different terms the words : "Who sees Me, sees the Father." This is the completely new and unique feature of Christianity, namely, that the objective presence of a fully human being is the key and the door to that which is fully divine. In none of the extra-Christian traditions, indeed, do spiritual way and divine truth coincide in the person of a historical man. The Buddha and the Hindu *guru* (spiritual master) indicate and follow the mystic way; Christ *is* the way. The prophets of monotheistic religions receive and proclaim the revealed truth; Christ *is* the Truth. These assertions constitute the foundation and the source of the pre-eminently Christian means of deification : " knowledge of faith. " The metaphysical East exalts knowledge as a means of spiritual development. Judaism and Islam emphasize faith as instrument of salvation. In either case, however, knowledge and faith are not only antinomic, but also heterogeneous. The characteristic of Christianity is to unite these two elements, without merging them, into a single spiritual act, a paradoxical act or movement which consists in penetrating to the very heart of the divine perspective through the mediacy of a human perspective. This characteristic has no equivalent outside Christianity, because the transparency of the " visible " to the " Invisible " is really infinite only in Christ, the only One of Whom it can be asserted : " God is that which Christ reveals [2]. "

In order to make clear the distinctive nature of the knowledge of faith, let it be remembered that the verb " to believe, " in Christian spirituality, has nothing in common with credulousness (whether the latter term is taken to denote a subjective conviction or an objective conjecture). We must not take " to believe " in the sense of " I believe it will rain tomorrow " or " I believe that you are right, " but in the sense it has in the statement " I believe you, " that is to say, " I make your viewpoint my own, " " I enter into your way of seeing men and things. " Faith is the specifically human ability to look at reality through the eyes of one's neighbor, through a " second self. " This ability really leads to a true knowledge, a direct intuition or perception, and not merely to a subjective feeling or inference; its immediate content, however, is not that which one's neighbor sees, but his person and the world as he sees it, his reality experienced by me in the " we. " It is a personal knowledge, whose characteristic is to be at the same

time inexhaustible and untranslatable in objective terms, because
such is the nature of its goal : the spiritual person. Spiritually
speaking, " to believe in an impersonal truth " has absolutely
no meaning.

When this other being, this neighbor, is the Person
of Christ, faith takes on a quality and a depth which
are inconceivable outside Christianity. Faith becomes the
ability to perceive through another man, albeit dimly, the
reality seen by God, and even — within the limits assigned to
humans — God in Person as He sees Himself. And all this
merely by looking through the eyes of Christ, by seeing " with "
Him. The knowledge of faith consists in gaining access to
the mystery of divine life by " putting on Christ " (*Gal.* 3 : 27),
by letting this mind be in us " which was also in Christ Jesus "
(*Phil.* 2 : 5); this knowledge consists in reaching the very center
of the God-Man and making His Heart the source of all our
actions.

### *God Incarnate, Supreme Antinomy and Total Synthesis.*

We would like to emphasize the completely unprecedented
nature of the God-Man as " incarnate Way, " in connection
with the opening verses, so deservedly famous, of the sacred
book of Chinese Taoism, the Tao-Te-King or " Book of the
Way and of Rectitude. " *Tao* means Principle and also Path;
as indicated by its ideograph, Tao designates total, transcendent
and omnipresent Reality, both as supreme origin and goal,
and as the way leading to this reality, or rather back to it. Now,
the first two verses immediately specify that " The path which
one can follow is not the true Path, the name which one can
utter is not the true Name [3]. " Traditionalists seeking to apply
these verses to Christianity will say that Christ is indeed
identical with this humanly inaccessible Way and this humanly
ineffable Name, but only in His divine nature, only in so far
as he coincides inwardly with the inaccessible Essence of God;

so that His coming into the world as man, far from being the sudden revelation of an unsuspected Truth denoting both a fulfillment and a new beginning, can only have been, as far as they are concerned, the confirmation and (as it were) the illustration of the eternal truth whose nature — forever inexpressible and *a fortiori* " unincarnatable " by definition — is precisely shown, in this view, by the Tao-Te-King. This constitutes a new form of the Monophysite heresy, which was tirelessly fought against by the early Church [4]. In this instance, it consists in rejecting as contradictory, and therefore as impossible, the antinomic mystery of the Incarnation, and hence in sweepingly denying that the Word could, through His very self-abasement, transcend (but without abolishing it) the " negative theology " of Taoism, in denying that He became flesh in order to reveal that the divine Essence is not ineffable Void, but Love, Love even to dying on the Cross. One can not overemphasize, and in this we agree with the Tao-Te-King, the fact that the names formulated by the very wisest of men and the paths open only to the most accomplished of ascetics have absolutely no common measure with the Name and the Way. But the Word, in becoming flesh, opened and made utterable through Grace, even to the least gifted of mortals, precisely this Way and this Name, naturally inaccessible and ineffable though they may be through man's most zealous personal contemplative efforts. That which is absolutely impossible to the human will ascending toward God, has become infinitely possible through the divine Will's descent toward man, on the one essential condition that man accept unreservedly this new dispensation. The Incarnation fulfills and transcends the deepest non-Christian intuitions, for the very reason which could but make it a " scandal " to the Jews and the Moslems, and a " folly " to the Greeks and the Orientals; namely, that God — His heart overflowing with love — expects from man no more than an infinitesimal but unconditional assent, in order to place within man's reach, so to speak, His infinite power. Zen Buddhism, in which the influence of Taoism is manifest, emphasizes so strongly the staggering disparity between human effort and spiritual " answer ", it stresses to such a degree the enlightening virtue of merely " letting go " to the fullest extent, that one may well wonder whether Zen is not closer than its commentators realize to what Christians call Grace.

In relation to such a new possibility, how should one evaluate the significance for the West of Eastern spirituality, and particularly of its specific dimension, interiority? In the economy of revelation, that which is unique can not be other than universal, and that which is new constitutes an implicit recapitulation. Human gateway opening onto the divine infinity, Christ includes and heightens incomparably more than He excludes and abolishes. He receives and transfigures every impulse toward God, the more so as this striving is more completely human, i. e., not only physical and psychic, but also and above all spiritual. Our encounter with the contemplative East therefore incites us to place on a deeper level of our being the starting point from which to fling ourselves into the deifying " mold " of the Word's humanity. This meeting with the East forces us to become newly aware of our essentially theocentric structure, to rediscover our " naturally supernatural " vocation, to call to mind again *why* " no man can say The Lord Jesus, but by the Holy Ghost " (I *Cor.* 12 : 3); thus, we are shown why it is not the soul of the traditional East, but truly that of the modern West, which has ceased to be *naturaliter christiana*.

The modern East, to the extent that it strives to imitate the present-day West, reminds us that nearly everything which happens around us has ceased to be Christian, except in name only. If our civilization, which is called upon to reflect the Face of the Father, were not generally Its caricature, the West would not have contributed to the perversion among our Oriental brethren of the very foundation of that " nature " which reaches completion and fulfillment through the Grace of Christ. But to attribute to our Christian heritage a responsibility which actually rests with the complete negation of Christianity, would aggravate our faithlessness still further. Whatever the errors committed in His name, Christ remains what He is : the Way and the Door. If the Word had not become flesh, the incontrovertible proof of the divine Absolute's irreducibly personal nature would be lacking. And without the ability to " clothe ourselves in " the Incarnate, we would not have the certainty that deification, far from gradually abolishing alterity or " presence of the Other as Other ", is on the contrary nourished by it, and that interiority can develop to the full only through participation in the Trinitarian mystery of the intradivine Life.

Transparent to the depths of God even in His body, the God-Man has restored to the human body the dignity which it possessed before the Fall. Original sin, indeed, does not consist in having fallen into the body, but in the fact that the body, with its opaque tendencies, gained dominance over the spirit, as soon as the latter separated itself from God. The hereditary disorder, the congenital obfuscation of the intellect resulting from this ascendency of the lower over the higher element, from this " interference " of the body and psyche in the spirit, affect the East as well as the West; they place both spiritual hemispheres under the painful necessity of *metanoia*, or " repentance, " i. e., the humiliating effort to repair or redress the original order of precedence within the human person. The Western reaction to this mortifying requirement, however, has been the complete opposite of the Eastern response. The Western materialist tries to avoid this obligation by exalting the body to the point of denying the reality of the spirit; and the Eastern " spiritualist " seeks to evade it by extolling the spirit to the extent of denying the reality of the body. Both mutilate the person [5]. Halfway between these two extremes, at the point where East and West both meet and diverge, rises the Cross of the New Adam; His Resurrection manifests and restores the body to its providential function as temple of the Spirit, " seat " both of the incommunicable personality and of the communication with the " other, " abode of interiority and, by the same token, gateway to transcendency, and thus itself also marked out for resurrection.

Before the Incarnation, interiority and transcendency, intellectual isolation and unitive love, appeared to be separated by an irreducible antinomy [6]; outside the Incarnation, East and West remain incompatible; " When the fullness of time had come, " however, this abyss was shown to be bridged as such within the Trinity and bridgeable within ourselves, because " God has sent into our hearts the Spirit of His Son, Who cries out : Abba, Father! "

### The Ambiguity of Traditionalism.

In concluding the first part of this study, we will draw the attention of traditionalists to a point which seems to have escaped them, by virtue of the very postulate preassumed in all their arguments [7]. Their aim is to extract the *in divinis* synthesis of all religions by proving that they are all derived from one original " revelation " or primordial " tradition. " Their purpose is consequently to embrace all religions within one great sweep of the mind, while still doing justice to the distinctive features of each. In order to fulfill the latter condition, which is actually a task beyond human possibilities, Traditionalists are forced to postulate, not only the transcendent unity of all religions, but also (through a subtle shift of emphasis) their ultimate equivalence in the eyes of God. Only this equivalence, or horizontal correspondence, allows them to assimilate, or rather to " homologate " the elements of one tradition to those of another, in accordance with the tendency which Mircea Eliade has observed in primitive and Oriental civilizations [8]; moving from one equivalence to another, they try in this way gradually to work their way back from the present multiplicity and distinction to the primordial unity, considered and postulated as original indistinction [9]. This clearly assumes that, between any two religions, there can exist at the most differences of degree, but never of nature.

What escapes the traditionalists is that this principle of " universal concordance, " of " transcendent equivalence " and " homologation, " is not a religious constant, but only an aspect of the nonmonotheistic traditions. The postulate in question, which has (as far as they are concerned) the value of an indisputable axiom, is perfectly compatible with the structure of extra-Biblical traditions, but is diametrically opposed to the specific nature of the Judeo-Christian revelation [10].

According to the most authoritative spokesmen for non-Biblical traditions, none of these claims to be the full revelation of God by and through Himself; each one of these traditions considers itself as a privileged, but not an absolute, expression of the Divinity; unique in its particulars, but not of its kind, each one translates into human mode (which is formal or conventional, and therefore fundamentally relative), rather than it reveals directly, the suprahuman, formless and radically inexpressible Truth also underlying other religions. As a matter of fact, this is what the parable of the elephant, which we have already analyzed, purports to establish and demonstrate. A Hindu, a Buddhist, a Taoist, or even a Sufi, remains perfectly within the bounds of orthodoxy when he considers other traditions as converging, in the same manner as his own, toward the same numinous Divinity which transcends them all in the same degree, and when he believes that each religion inevitably conceals as much as it reveals. It is true that devout Orientals holding these views are in a minority; far from being heterodox, however, they constitute the religious elite, next to which the less tolerant majority of the faithful appears as a relatively unenlightened exoteric element. To profess a non-Biblical religion as being the only and the full revelation would thus be tantamount, and the traditionalists have seen this clearly, to mistaking a part for the whole, which is a criterion of heresy, and to falling prey to an arrogant exclusivism. The structure of Oriental traditions is such that, the more we grasp one of them *ab intra*, the more everything which distinguishes it from other nonmonotheistic traditions seems to fade away; so that they all ultimately coincide through their common Center, in this metacosmic, omnipresent and forever unrevealable Reality which Rudolf Otto calls the " Numinous, " root of the " Sacred [11]. "

The exact opposite is true of the Biblical revelation, and *a fortiori* of Christianity, which is the supreme fulfillment of the Bible's promises. The more the self-revelation of God as absolute and infinite Person (i. e., as Holy) asserts itself, or the more it allows itself to be apprehended *ab intra*, the less it can be confused with other religions. It must of necessity be so, because the Holy, God in Person, the " Holy Father " of the sacerdotal prayer of Christ, is all the more Himself as He is not the " alien gods " (and the latter designation includes the impersonal Deity). The order of Holiness, corollary of the direct revelation, is all the less reducible to the order of the Sacred as the former becomes more distinct from the latter : the Holy, indeed, goes beyond the Sacred, while " assuming " it in an entirely new dimension which God alone could manifest. The Judeo-Christian tradition never incorporates the religious features or aspects of the civilizations within which it develops by means of " homologation, " but always through " conversion. "

Therefore, and this is what traditionalists cannot or will not see, when a Christian professes that his religion embodies the only full revelation, he is only expressing in other words the fact that Christ is the Only Son of God, " in Whom dwells the fullness of the Divinity. " The Christian does not take this stand through any kind of parochialism, but simply because it is impossible for him to formulate his faith in any other way, or to restrict even slightly this foundation of his faith, without by the same token ceasing to be a Christian. Traditionalists praise the open-mindedness of Vishnuism, which allows its faithful to equate Christ to a ninth *avatâra* of Vishnu, and hence to "another Krishna." But they fail to notice that what is gained in width is lost in depth, when one thus grasps only a semblance or imitation of Christ, which actually conceals Him from our eyes. And traditionalists lament the exclusiveness of the Christian faith, which obviously forbids equating Krishna to "another Only Son" of God, without even suspecting that this seeming restriction actually constitutes a gain in depth, as well as in width. They fail to see that this Christian "No," when correctly explicited, and because it illuminates the "vertical" transcendency of the Holy in relation to the Sacred, endows the inner eye with this "theandric breadth of vision," thanks to which one can precisely do full justice to the mystical originality of the "Song of the Lord" devoted to the eighth *avatâra* of Vishnu, where there occasionally transpires something like a nostalgia for true holiness. Traditionalists reject this "perspective" *a priori* because it implies a real confrontation of the creature with the Creator, and because their basic postulate does not — as they are well aware — hold up to this confrontation. This calls for a few final words of explanation.

The monotheistic God is absolute. He does not relate to anything, even when considered as Person. Personal in Himself, He is also personifying as Creator of man. He made man in His own image so as to enter, once for all, into a reciprocal relationship with His creature. Hence, it is not enough to say, with the nonmonotheistic traditions, that man must be "in his depth" in order to reach the Divine; it is necessary to add that man must be before God, facing his Creator — *in conspectu Dei* — in order to reach his ultimate depth. Only then will God lead man back to himself by showing him his irreducible personal center, where interiority is inseparably linked to transcendency, and which is the image of God in man [12]. There only will man, receiving in the divine Presence the Call of his Creator, find himself responsible toward God and free in the full sense of the word. He can then no longer, in good faith, " homologate " the Creator to an impersonal principle of manifestation, nor Revelation in time to the immemorial Tradition, nor Divine Unity to the original indistinction; man then senses how fallacious is the equivalence *in divinis* of Christian love and *bhakti* or *maitrî*, of monotheistic faith and intellectual intuition, of the sin of Adam and the cosmic illusion; man then perceives, albeit dimly, the fundamental difference between sage and saint, deliverance and resurrection, between the realization of the Self through denial of the ego and the humble love which sets free and sanctifies. And if he answers the call of the God of Abraham — " Adam, where art thou? " —, he sees that the non-Biblical traditions have exhausted all the analogies linking the microcosm and the macrocosm to the Divine Principle, save one : that of man himself as personal and indissoluble image of the Living God. And he understands that all the equivalences or homologations between these traditions and the Judeo-Christian revelation can but mask the true face of Christ.

If Christ were not the only complete revelation, if He were but one manifestation among many of the Truth, albeit the most sublime, He would not be Christ. Among all religions, Christianity is the only one which must be either total Truth or wild imposture. There is no middle course. A " homologable " Christianity would not be one religion among others, but would fade away into pure fantasy. It is " incomparable " or it is nothing.

Clearly, the traditionalist postulate thus defeats its own purpose — i. e., the metaphysical synthesis of *all* religions — since it excludes Biblical monotheism from this synthesis, through the very attempt to include it *ab extra*.

The ardent wish to make mankind better and happier through the unification of all religions is one thing; and fervent intercession for the union of all souls in the sanctifying love of the revealed God is another. In our time, the former purpose may quite possibly constitute Lucifer's most subtle attempt to bring about the failure of the latter.

\* \*
\*

[1] Concerning the antinomic outlook of the Greek Fathers, see *Théologie Mystique de l'Eglise d'Orient*, by Vladimir Lossky (Aubier, Paris), and in particular pp. 23, 29, 41 and 75. The entire writings of Saint Augustine are imbued with this same spirit, which is, indeed, that of all the Saints (cf., for instance, the " Ignatian sentence " quoted below, Part II, Chapter IV, Footnote 4). It is the very spirit of the Scriptures, of the incarnate Word. — In his study entitled *La Théologie de la Lumière selon saint Grégoire de Thessalonique* (Dieu Vivant, 1946), Vladimir Lossky asserts that a dogma appears whenever two truths, which seem mutually exclusive, are both equally revealed.

[2] *Foi et Connaissance*, by August Brunner (Munich 1951), a remarkable analysis from which we have drawn the central idea developed in the two following paragraphs. By the same author : *Die Religion* (Freiburg, Herder, 1956).

[3] Literally : " Way can follow not true (or eternal) way, name can utter not true name. "

[4] At the opposite extreme from Nestorianism, which denies the unity of the Person of Christ, let us recall that Monophysism denies the actual distinction between His two natures in favor of the divine nature only. Left to its own devices, human thought inevitably swings back and forth between these two " poles " of heterodoxy, without ever being able to reconcile them. Cf. Part II below, Chapter IV, p. 143. Russian theologians feel justified in accusing Western Christians of " Jesuanism " or " spiritual Nestorianism, " and the latter reproach the Christian East with its " pneumatism " or " mystical Monophysism. " Actually, the propensity for these two extremes typifies first and foremost our fallen nature as such (human thought when not " in a state of Grace "), and only to a lesser degree particular races, traditions or Churches. It is

vain to attempt to restore the unity of the Church by attacking either of
these extremes in one's brethren, before having fought against their common
root in oneself.

⁵ We will return to this point in Chapter IV of Part II, under the
heading " Quietism and Voluntarism, two conjugate extremes " (p. 123).
Since any extreme inevitably produces its antithesis, what we say above
(about the two opposite " reactions " before the need for repentance)
does not contradict, but on the contrary explains, the fact that the East
has its Quietist " materialism, " and the West its voluntarist or Pelagian
forms of " spiritualism. "

⁶ In Part II (p. 140 ff.), we will refer to another antinomy, the terms
of which can be reconciled, without being confused or destroyed, only
through participation in Christ. These terms are " negative " (or apophatic)
theology, which prevails in the Christian East, and " affirmative " (or
cataphatic) theology, which predominates in the Latin church.

⁷ See in particular Frithiof Schuon : *De l'unité transcendante des
Religions* (Gallimard). The title already indicates the postulate which we
will discuss; as confirmed by the book itself, it preassumes the existence
of a metaphysical viewpoint prior and superior to all religious " perspectives. " The author develops the fundamental thesis of René Guénon.

⁸ Cf. his *Traité de l'Histoire des Religions*. The Brahmins, for instance,
have equated, or rather " homologated, " the Vedic sacrifice to yoga,
by considering the latter as an " inner sacrifice. "

⁹ Quite evidently, a supreme Reality conceived of as complete
indistinction can only be impersonal : being only on the threshold of the
metacosmic " holy distance " which infinitely separates the world from
God, it is not absolutely transcendent. — In this context, we will point
out that the Vedantine equation $âtmâ = Brahma$ is but a speculative reduction
to unity of the countless Vedic equivalences or correlations, which are
ritual in nature, between the human microcosm and the universal
macrocosm. These equivalences are converted into a supreme identity
through a " passage to the limit " carried out by the Brahmins during the
post-Vedic period of the Upanishads. (In this connection, consult Louis
Renou, whose views are condensed by Olivier Lacombe in the latter's
above-mentioned article, published in *La Revue Thomiste*).

Regarding the fundamental " Impersonalism " of the divine
" Principle, " see Frithiof Schuon, *op. cit.*, Chapter III, Section 3.

¹⁰ We have deliberately omitted Islam, although it is derived from
the Abrahamic tradition, because Islamic Sufism, at least in its intellectual

and plotinizing form, is " concordist, " in spite of the fact that it is founded upon Koranic orthodoxy. Cf. *The Idea of Personality in Sufism*, by R.-A. Nicholson.

[11] Cf. *Das Heilige* (The Holy), by Rudolf Otto. The title is misleading. As we are trying to show, it would be preferable to call this book *Das Sakrale* (The Sacred). Regarding the specific essence of " the Holy, " we refer to the works of Dietrich von Hildebrand, and in particular : *Transformation in Christ* (New York, Longmans, Green, 1948), *Liturgy and Personality* (New York, Longmans, Green, 1943), *Pureté et Virginité* (translated into French from the original German, Paris, Desclée de Brouwer, 1947), and *Christian Ethics* (see below, Conclusion of Part II, Footnote 36). Nobody has emphasized better than he the personalizing power and sanctifying beauty of moral values as " theophanies " revealed by and in the incarnate Word.

[12] The person is immortal, indissoluble, and irreducible to a " thing, " because it is made in the image of "the only 'Thou' which by essence cannot possibly become a ' That. ' " Martin Buber, quoted by Henry de Lubac in *Sur les Chemins de Dieu* (Aubier), p. 118.

*Part II*

# The Hesychast Method
of Prayer and its Spiritual
Significance in the Borderland
between East and West.

Animae et carnis adunatio assumens Spiritum Patris, hominem spiritualem perficit.

Saint IRENAEUS,
(Adv. Haereses, V, 6, 1)

# Introductory Remarks

We will complete the preceding study with an analysis of Hesychasm, or Russo-Byzantine mysticism, and its method of prayer : the " Prayer of the Heart, " also known as " Prayer of Jesus. " This method, which was developed at Mount Athos and to which the spirituality of the Eastern Church owes its distinctive quality, consists essentially in making the intelligence descend into the heart, in order to introduce the Name of Jesus therein, by means of the repeated invocation, timed to follow the respiratory rhythm, of a formula containing this Name. Hesychasm appears to occupy a position midway between the spiritual techniques of the non-Christian East and the mystical methods or spiritual exercises practiced within the Church of Rome. After an outline of the cosmological and metaphysical basis of Hesychasm, *Analogy-Participation* [1] (Chapter 1), we will examine one of its features — whose affinity to truly Oriental spiritualities the reader will easily recognize — namely " enstasy, " as opposed to " ecstasy " (Chapter 2), in order to draw out its fundamentally Christian dimension : the eminently " received " and " freely given " nature of Hesychast deification (Chapter 3). We will close this study by considering the dangers, the limitations and the value of the Hesychast method, with special emphasis on the twin

pitfalls of Quietism and Prometheism, and on the risk of
Angelism (Chapter 4). Since Hesychasm attempts to incorporate
essentially non-Monotheistic practices and perspectives into
Christian *theôsis*, these critical considerations continue the
conclusion to the first part of the present work.

* * *

[1] We borrow this term from the valuable study devoted by Vladimir
Lossky to *La notion des " analogies " chez Denys le pseudo-Aréopagyte* (Archives
d'histoire doctrinale et littéraire du moyen-âge), V (1931), pp. 279-309.
See also his penetrating *Essai sur la théologie mystique de l'Eglise d'Orient*
(Aubier 1943), Chapter VI : Image et Ressemblance.

# Analogy-Participation, the Metaphysical Basis of Hesychast Deification or *Theôsis*.

I

"Where the body is, there also should be the intellect." "A Hesychast is an incorporeal being... who strives to confine his soul in its corporeal abode" by "making the intelligence descend into the heart." Now, "breathing is the natural way to the heart; having gathered your intellect within yourself... force it, together with the air you inhale, to descend into your heart and remain there... You are to understand, moreover, that once your intelligence is firmly established in your heart, it is not to remain silent and inactive, but must unceasingly repeat the prayer: 'Lord Jesus Christ, Son of God, have mercy upon me!'" "At first one experiences nothing but grief and darkness, but before long one perceives a kind of light." Thereafter, as soon as an evil thought arises, and even before being completed and fully taking shape, it is expelled and annihilated through the invocation of the Name of Jesus [1]. Light, warmth, sweetness, tears and peace are the "tokens" that the Name called upon has entered into one's heart.

This summary of the Hesychast method, i. e., of the use — so much debated in the West — of psychophysical means in order to facilitate the sharply focused invocation of the Name of Jesus, is borrowed from the Russian version of the Philokalia, a compendium of what the Saints of the Desert, the Greek Fathers, and the masters of Byzantine spirituality have said and written about the Prayer of the Heart [2]. Although the " perpetual prayer " appears in the Rule of Saint Basil, the Father of Eastern Monasticism (Great Rule 37), and is described by Cassian (that connecting link between the Christian East and the Christian West), it was not included in the Rule of Saint Benedict, the Father of Western Monasticism. The use of the complete traditional formula cited above has been recorded as early as the sixth Century. " The prayer itself is called ' secret meditation ' and is said to be transmitted by the older monks to the younger, through a kind of personal and oral initiation. The secret nature of this prayer may explain why it is never quoted in full by early theological commentators, who considered it to be part of a secret tradition [3]. "

Be that as it may, the invocation of the Name of Jesus, whether through the *Monologistos* or in a more developed orison, does not seem to have been formally handed down in the Latin Church. The impression of utter novelty which it made on the theologians who rediscovered it a thousand years later confirms this hypothesis. There is therefore nothing surprising about the initial reactions against Hesychasm, of which at first the Latin tradition received only a caricature. But how is it that, even after the West had the opportunity to form a true estimate of this method, the opinion prevailed that this " technique " of contemplation was incompatible with the Christian conception of Grace? If it were a question of Mohammedan *Dhikr* or Hindu *Yoga*, whose similarity, incidentally, to the technical aspect of Hesychasm is undeniable, this opinion could be explained by the wish to avoid introducing any extraneous element into Christian prayer; but when it comes to a method tested (as far as its original core is concerned, at any rate) by an uninterrupted line of Christian ascetics going back to the Desert Fathers [4], the mistrust shown by the West calls for an explanation, which must first be sought in a difference of approach and emphasis. We shall then examine whether or not this divergence affects the essence of Christianity.

## Convergence or Divergence of Nature and Grace?

We believe that this divergence arises from the manner in which the Christian East and West each consider the relationship between nature and Grace. As far as the former is concerned, there cannot possibly be such a thing as " pure " nature, isolated from Grace, because Grace is implied in Creation, in such a way that Creation is " naturally supernatural; " Latin theology, on the other hand, — particularly since its well-founded reaction against Baianism, which saw in Grace an integral part of nature — considers Grace as foreign to Creation, and at times even has a tendency to conceive of the whole supernatural order not only as superimposed, but as " superadded " to, the natural order [5]. Father Pegon, S. J. (in his introduction to the French translation of Saint Maximus the Confessor's *Centuries on Charity*, p. 43), has this to say on the subject : " While in the West, from relatively early times, ' nature, ' as distinguished from ' Grace ' or ' supernature, ' designates a principle of life and a fundamental human tendency which is more or less ' antisupernatural, ' Maximian spirituality seems to recognize in *Physis* and *hyper Physin* two phases of a single development. Nature — for Saint Maximus as for most of the Greek Fathers — is man as image of God, i. e., the abstract nature of our theologians plus their ' preternatural gifts. ' In the language of Western spirituality, therefore, ' to follow nature ' means to run ' counter ' to Grace; but for Saint Maximus the same words denote striving ' with ' Grace to restore the divine image. Our nature is very nearly the law of sin; for Saint Maximus, it designates roughly what we require of Grace ... As to the qualification ' supernatural, ' it is reserved for that which directly concerns deification. "

It can be seen that Hesychasm is but the methodical application of the Maximian viewpoint. If nature in general is ordered in accordance with the supernatural to the point of reaching completion in it and of culminating, so to speak, in deifying Grace, then it is clear that human nature, in its dual quality of microcosm — or summary of Creation — and of God's image — or reflection of the Creator —, must necessarily be so constituted as to form, even in its bodily structure, a springboard from which one may become aware of Grace, a temple of the Holy Spirit, a foundation for deification. Between the bodily modalities of consciousness, its spiritual modalities, and their transcendent principle, there must accordingly exist, not merely accidental, miraculous and unintelligible contacts, but an analogical relationship, established by the " divine economy, " an organic connection; the Hesychast method aims precisely at changing this connection or inner continuity from a potentiality into an actuality, starting in particular with the two vital functions of breathing and action of the heart, whose interdependence was well known, even in Antiquity. The relationship between the inhaled or inspired " breath " and the Spirit (*Pneuma*, the " divine Breath ") is then much more than a metaphor; it constitutes a real, " analogical " correspondence, making of the former the providential vehicle of the latter. The same " vertical " connection links the heart, physical center and " sun " of the body, to the intellect *(noûs)*, spiritual center and light of the soul, and by the same token to God, the increate Light, metaphysical Center and Heart of the universe, to use the words of Gregory Palamas, Maximus the Confessor and Clement of Alexandria. According to Saint Gregory of Nyssa, the heart, " image of the image " (i. e., image of the *noûs*, God's mirror in man), becomes " God's abode " to the extent that man lives " in the physical heart, but not physically " (Theophanus the Recluse), that is, to the extent that corporeal consciousness and incorporeal consciousness, simultaneously centered in the heart and in the intellect, coincide through their increate center. It is now recognized that for the Christian East, faithful to the Scriptures and to the tradition of Antiquity, the " heart " is not only the seat of affective life (as so often believed in the modern West, in spite of the teachings of Cassian and Saint Augustine), but also constitutes that of the intelligence. Nevertheless, it must be made clear that, in Hesychasm, the intelligence thus associated with the heart is not discursive reason *(dianoia)*, symbolically located in the brain, but the intellect *(noûs)*, the spiritual organ created for contemplation in the dual sense of illuminating knowledge and unitive love, the intuitive faculty directed, not toward the rational principle of contradiction or sufficient reason, but toward the spiritual principle of " coincidence of opposites " in the " divine darkness. " The *noûs* — or *intellectus*, which Saint Thomas, also, distinguished from *ratio* — transcends and includes the mental as well as the sentimental faculties; " equidistant " from these two sets of faculties, the *noûs* as conceived of by Hesychasm is their common spiritual root, just as the heart is analogically the vital root of their respective symbolic locations : the brain and the bowels. There is, then, between spiritual and bodily organisms, an exact correspondence, a rigorous analogy in the Dionysian sense of " effective participation " (of the lower in the higher orders) and of " *reciprocal communion :* " gathered in the " middle of the heart " as in an inextended center, the bodily sensations, which are ordinarily diffuse and " deifugal " as a result of original sin, contribute — in this view — to the recollection of the powers of the soul in the *noûs*, and help to bring about the unification of the total consciousness in the Holy Spirit; and the illumination of the heart-spirit by the Spirit, in turn, is capable of " consuming the materiality of the heart " (Callixtus and Ignatius) [6]; cut off from the Spirit, on the other hand, the intellect would lose its intuition of universal realities (the vision of divine Ideas) and would gradually become attached to the egocentric mental images (the *eidôla*) which make of the " carnal self " the intellect's prison. The body should consequently become detached from this psychic activity which makes it insensitive to the universal realities by " intercepting " them, and should take root in the intellect so as to become the temple of the Spirit. Thus considered, the body is naturally ordered to that " transmutation of the senses " which Gregory Palamas speaks of, and which, in the case of Saints, brings about, even in this life, the transformation, mentioned by Saint Paul, of the " physical body " into the " spiritual body. "

This " analogy-participation " also governs all the orders of creation, according to Dionysius, for God's invisible attributes are " understood by the things that are made " (*Rom.* 1 : 20).

### *Prayer Considered as Inner Eucharist.*

It may be objected that the preceding pages, while they do indeed show that the providential analogy of nature and supernature is traditional in the Christian East, do not however prove the actual existence of such an analogy. To which a Hesychast would answer as follows : had God made Himself spirit, one might argue the matter; now, would the human body have been capable of serving as a temple for Divinity if nature as such were " antisupernatural? " The Word was made flesh, certainly not because God is anthropomorphic, but quite possibly, it would seem, because man is Theomorphic. " Disclosing what remained veiled in the doctrine of Moses, " has the Incarnation not put a finishing touch to our nature (which is made in the image of God); has it not thus revealed, and hence manifested, our Christocentric structure? Hesychasm takes literally, so to speak, the fact that, since the Incarnation, every true " analogy " has become a " Christology. " In this context, " to clothe oneself in Christ " would consist less in " imitating " Him than in " interiorizing " Him, i. e., in *becoming aware* of our potential connaturality with the God-Man by " actualizing " the total Presence of God to Himself in His Son; the " transformation in Christ " would not be so much the application to man of the merits of the Incarnation and Redemption, as the continuation in man of the

Incarnation itself, in so far as it is perpetuated by the Eucharistic mystery. And calling someone by name — would add our Hesychast — causes this person to become present. Thanks to analogy-participation, the fervent and concentrated invocation of the Name of Jesus " in the heart " is therefore, in the views of Hesychasm, an extension of the Incarnation, an " inner Eucharist : " through this conscious and deliberate invocation of the name of Jesus, says the Philokalia, " the heart absorbs the Lord, and the Lord absorbs the heart. " The introduction into the heart of the " Name which passeth all names " would therefore enable our original deiformity to progress from " image " to " resemblance " — from intermittent memory to continuous state. " God is present to all things, " says Dionysius the Areopagite, " but all things do not remain present to Him; " he adds that, by means of the Prayer of the Heart, man — and through him the world — returns to God's presence. God's presence to the world (called " presence of immensity ") and God's presence to man (called " presence of habitation ") seem, from the point of view of fallen nature, to oppose and exclude each other; they converge, on the contrary, in the measure that the soul is re-established in Grace; and the more the heart is illuminated by the Spirit (which transcends the universe and man *ab intra*), the more it sees the vastness of the former join the intensity of the latter; both coincide in the total Presence (called " presence of the hypostatic union "). It is true that total Presence belongs by right only to Christ; but has not Saint Paul exhorted us to " attain the full stature of Christ? " To clothe oneself in the Second Adam, is this not to complete with Him the cosmogonical design which was interrupted by the transgression of the first Adam? Is it not to co-operate in the transfiguration of time and space, in the coming of the eternal Eighth Day when " God shall be all in all? " According to the Philokalia, such then, thanks to analogy-participation, is the supreme end of the " Prayer of the Heart " or " Hesychast orison, " whose full perfection produces a state wherein the prayer, having become continuous, " springs effortlessly from the heart, even during heavy sleep, " a state in which Saint Paul's exclamation " It is no longer I who live, but Christ Who lives in me " has become like a second nature.

We have seen that Hesychasm appears to be a sort of " synthesis " between the two poles of all human spirituality, interiority and transcendency, whose respective predominance, as we have shown in our study of "The Encounter of Religions," seems to characterize the East and the West. Everything takes place as if Hesychasm aspired to reconcile, by integrating them to the incarnate Word, these two apparently incompatible modes of contemplation : on the one hand and in the broader sense, Oriental spirituality, whose extreme form is the Hindu doctrine of interiorization of the universe and restoration through knowledge of the " Self, " conceived of as identical with the " suprapersonal " Deity; and on the other hand, Latin mysticism, governed by the union of the creature, made out of nothing, with the absolute transcendency of the personal God. We will now describe how Hesychasm has utilized these wo modes as two complementary phases of *Theôsis*.

*  *
 *

[1] Summary of the *Methodos* (Hesychast treatise ascribed to Saint Simeon the New Theologian) taken from *La Prière de Jésus*, by " Un Moine de l'Eglise d'Orient " (Editions de Chevetogne, 1951), p. 39.

[2] Cf. *Writings from the Philokalia on the Prayer of the Heart*, translated from the Russian Text " Dobrotolubiye, " by E. Kadloubovsky and G. E. H. Palmer (Faber and Faber, London 1951). Cf. also the bibliography appearing at the beginning of *Prière du Cœur*, by Jacques-Albert Cuttat, under the pseudonym H. de B. (Editions Orthodoxes, Paris 1953), the *Petite Philocalie de la Prière du Cœur* (Editions des Cahiers du Sud, Paris 1953), translated by Jean Gouillard, and *Contribution Orthodoxe*, by the Hieromonk Antoine Bloom, in *Technique et Contemplation*, Etudes Carmélitaines, pp. 49 ff.

[3] Hieromonk Basil Krivochein, of the Mount Athos Monastery of Saint Panteleimon : *Date du Texte traditionnel de la " Prière de Jésus, "* Messager de l'Exarchat du Patriarche Russe, 1951, 7-8, p. 54.

[4] In reviewing the original French edition of the present book, *(Revue de l'Histoire des Religions,* October-December 1958 issue, pp. 246-247), Antoine Guillaumont makes the following comments regarding this early " testing " of Hesychast methods : " It may be advisable to distinguish between the *monologistos* prayer itself (the invocation of the name of Jesus) and the accompanying techniques of concentration found in Hesychast texts. In any case, and in the present state of our knowledge concerning the spirituality of the early Eastern Church, it does not seem possible to answer this question (whether the Desert Fathers actually practiced the Prayer of Jesus) one way or the other with any degree of certainty. And our final opinion of the Western ' attitude ' toward the Hesychast orison depends to a large extent on the answer which this question will receive. "

[5] See Henri de Lubac : *Surnaturel,* Aubier 1946, especially pp. 375 ff.

[6] According to a contemporary Athonite monk, spiritual tears — fruit of the " gift of tears " — are the *sign* of the union of intellect and heart. It is an example of the participation of the body in the life of the spirit in a fully unified consciousness.

# 2

# The First Phase of *Theôsis* : Enstasy or "Isolation" Through Interiorization, Eastern Component of Hesychasm.

The "Eastern" mode, i.e., extreme interiorization of consciousness, appears in the first phase, which actually coincides with the Hesychast method proper; we recognize in it most of the elements of the mysticism which is called "natural" (retraction of the senses, invocation timed to the rhythm of breathing, reabsorption of consciousness into the heart, impassiveness, intellectual illumination, gentle and luminous warmth experienced in the heart, integration of the outer world), [1] all of which, in reality, are but aids to concentration. This method, which aims at emptying the intellect of all thought, image, and passion in order to return it to its original character of "mirror of God" in the "abyss of the heart," stems from an idea without which it is impossible to understand the methods of concentration presenting a "technical" structure; we refer to the idea that the meeting with God could not be achieved by starting from fallen nature as such, but presupposes the preliminary restoration of our Adamic nature : a nature injured (but not destroyed) by original sin, a nature "hidden under the fog of our passions," but which nevertheless "subsists fully, just as it was created" (Saint Simeon). The spiritual ascent, therefore, should begin, not by an impulse toward God and outward from oneself, an "excentric" movement — which constitutes the meaning of the word " ecstasy, " as used by Evagrius Ponticus —, but on the contrary by a return to and a re-entering into oneself, an " enstasy. " The first stage can only be a " concentric " movement, in relation to the mind warped by the hereditary *prelest* (*planê*, the inveterate tendency to " illusion, " to " false imputation, " to " circumscribing the divinity within figures and forms, " in the words of Evagrius). Enstasy starts with a " withdrawal " *ad intra* before the ego which has been perverted by our congenital acquiescence in original sin, with a *metanoia*. This term is usually translated as " repentance; " it actually means " sudden intellectual change. " The same word also denotes the sacrament of penance, precisely because, for Hesychasm, repentance should penetrate to the intellectual root of our mental, volitional, and affective faculties, since this sacrament, which restores us to the state of baptismal Grace and by the same token to our Adamic purity, has the power of making us " feel intensely the supernatural splendor of our soul " (Saint Gregory of Sinai), of showing us our original " identity with the celestial light of our incorruptible archetype " (Saint Macarius). The deifying ascent (the eucharist-state), under penalty of becoming an illusion in the eyes of Hesychasm, must be preceded by the *metanoia*-state, on the same grounds and for the same reasons that confession must precede and not follow communion.

### The Search for the Place of the Heart.

After this explanation, it will be understood why a work attributed to one of the highest authorities on this subject, Saint Simeon the New Theologian, far from recommending the first two of the three " methods of attention and of orison " which it describes, affective prayer and mental prayer (improperly called " prayer of the spirit " by Latin mystical theology), energetically warns against the psychic dangers and the risks of *prelest* which they entail. Saint Simeon sanctions only the

third method, the Prayer of the Heart, which he relates to the
Sermon on the Mount. In the first place, he writes, one must
" search diligently for the place of the heart. " And he adds :
" This is where the war begins " (the revolt of the passions
in the heart). While moral repentance follows the consciousness
of sin, Hesychast repentance precedes, as it were, and elicits
it, because it arises from the preaffective and prediscursive
center of one's being. " Impassiveness *(apatheia)* does not
consist in the absence of passions, but in their rejection "
(Centuries of Callixtus and Ignatius). The *apathos* monk differs
from others not through ataraxy, but through this fruit of
spiritual concentration : discernment of the spirit, the ability
to see evil even before being tempted to commit it. In order
to clarify this idea, we might say that God remains outside
us in the measure that the passions (including the mental passions)
are within us, i. e., in so far as we unknowingly identify ourselves
with the " dark spirits which dwell somewhere near the heart "
(Diadochus of Photike). If the characteristic of the devil is to
deny his existence, the characteristic of Christian ascetic doctrine
is to force our deifugal tendencies to " objectify " themselves,
so that the mere presence of a Saint (in whom repentance takes
on a sacrificial aspect) is capable of communicating to those
who approach him the " absolving " consciousness of their
unworthiness, just as the mere nearness of the Redeemer aroused
in the blind man of Jericho the spontaneous appeal for mercy
which became the formula of the Prayer of the Heart.

### *The Contemplative Integration of the Cosmos.*

The first phase of *theôsis* in turn is subdivided into
two " stages, " the first of which we have just described. The
Greek Fathers called them respectively *praxis* or *praktikê*
(practice of the purgative virtues centered in *enkrateia* or " mastery
of self "), and *physikê theôria :* the " contemplation *(theôria)*
of the nature of things *(physis)* " or " contemplative cosmology. "

The first, withdrawal into the " naked intellect " *(noûs gymnos)*,
is like the negative side of the second. *Praxis*, says Origen,
is an ascent toward *theôria*. The first corresponds to baptism,
the second to confirmation. Having become lucid again
*(diagnostikos)* through the " purification of the intellect, the
soul, and the body, " the *intelligence* discerns " the divine wisdom
invisibly contained in creatures " (Saint Maximus); it recovers
the intuitive vision of things as they are, as Adam saw them
before the Fall had made his concepts completely " externa-
lizing. " The newly cleared intelligence sees things " from
within, " in their " essence aspiring and straining toward God "
*(theotelês logos)*. In spite of appearances, the reintegration of
the center does not narrow the field of consciousness, but
on the contrary widens it. Everything takes place, in this
interiorized " cosmic liturgy ², " as though the universe had
ceased to be external to the one whose " purified heart becomes
an interior sky, with its own sun, moon, and stars, and
circumscribes God, the Uncircumscribable, by the secret ascent
of his vision " (Philotheus of Sinai). On the authority of the
words " heaven and earth shall pass away, but My words *(logoi
moû)* shall not pass away, " Evagrius Ponticus and Saint Maximus
the Confessor assert that the proper object of *physikê theôria*
is precisely that which, in the universe, does not pass away;
namely, the *logoi* — " unchanging essences " or " creative
words " — of things, the world as aspect of the divine *Logos*,
the universe as God pronounces it through the very Word
Whose Name is invoked in the heart. According to the Greek
Fathers, the relationship between the real essence and the
transitory surface of things is the same as the relationship between
the spirit and the letter of Holy Scripture, for the universe
is a book in which God's words may be read, and Holy Scripture
is the universe as God thinks it. Saint Maximus states that
it is essential to assimilate, by imitating them, the rhythms
and lessons of the *liber mundi;* to conform, as does the sun,
" to every event . . ., without forsaking any of one's own

illuminating identity, " to " gather up the spiritual *logoi* of other beings, " not in order to appropriate them, but " in order to offer them on behalf of creation as gifts to God. " Here prayer becomes " participation in universal existence " (according to the definition of a contemporary Athonite monk), where " the heart is aflame with love for every creature " (Saint Macarius), where knowledge blossoms into " cosmic charity; " where the " presence of habitation " develops into the " presence of immensity, " as the universe becomes more transparent to the increate Light of the Word invoked in the heart.

At the end of this second stage, and therefore also of the first phase of *theôsis,* " the soul, although still remaining the same soul, like a red hot iron, can no longer be touched by anything external. " Now, " the more one mysteriously enters into the light of knowledge, " says Saint Simeon, the more one is " ineffably plunged into a total unknowing, " and " the more God shines in the spirit, the more He becomes invisible. " The divine Essence is unknowable or " *unobjectifiable,* " and therefore is fundamentally interior. God is never the " object " of knowledge, not because His infinity is exterior, but because His interiority is infinite. And indeed He reveals Himself as the Subject of knowledge in the measure that the intellect regains its " proper state " *(katastasis toû noû)* in which, according to Evagrius, the vision of God becomes one with the vision of self.

\* \* \*

[1] Very significant in this respect is the title of a penetrating study published in the special number of *Cahiers du Sud,* devoted to Yoga (1953) : *L'Hésychasme . . . yoga chrétien?,* by the Hieromonk Antoine Bloom.

[2] We borrow the phrase " cosmic liturgy " *(liturgie cosmique)* from the title of a book by Hans Urs von Balthasar, devoted to the spirit of the Greek Fathers. (Cf. note 6, page 34 of the present study).

# 3

# The Second Phase of *Theôsis :*
# " Received Identity, "
# the Properly Christian Component
# of Hesychasm.

The typically " Oriental " flavor of the
preceding quotations might cause one to believe that the endlessly
concentric movement of Hesychast contemplation culminates
in a coincidence with God or, in other words, a reabsorption
into God of our innermost identity. However, at the very
point where the two modes of spirituality with which we are
concerned — those of Hesychasm and of the non-Christian
Orient — converge the most, Hesychast *theôsis* opens onto
the pre-eminently Christian or Monotheistic dimension, namely
the irreducible transcendency of the personal God, while
" Oriental " contemplation follows its course into an uninterrupted deepening and an unbroken stabilization of concentric
recollection. Indeed, the latter proceeds toward a " transcendency " which continues and unfailingly completes the
process of interiorization as such; its goal is not so much to
obtain deifying Grace, *dei-ficatio*, as to gain awareness of an
identity which has never really ceased to be divine [1].

## From the Impersonal Deity to the Living God.

This is not to say that the non-Christian forms of
asceticism are ignorant of the divine Transcendency and
Personality, as some have claimed. Nevertheless, they consider
the second as a " nonsupreme " facet of the first, an aspect
which will eventually fade away, when knowledge rises to

the original Non-Duality. Indeed, no trace of otherness, be it even divine Otherness, can subsist in the face of a knowledge conceived of as realizing the supreme identity, i.e., as an innate light dispelling by degrees the illusory distinction between knowing subject and known object, on all levels of reality, including the penultimate, so to speak (the level where Reality still wears the distinctive aspect of " the Lord " because, according to Oriental metaphysics, the knowing subject itself is still clothed in its ultimate "personal" envelope.) In the view of Oriental metaphysics, the God Person is not God in Himself, as an intradivine relation. He is God only in relation to the world and to man, which means that He too is relative and, in the final analysis, illusory. In this view, as we have already seen, ultimate and unconditioned reality is reserved for a " suprapersonal " Absolute, " transcendent " and yet accessible, because creatures and things are no more than its modalities or "modifications," i.e., necessary manifestations of which God would fundamentally be only the other face, the true essence into which everyone and everything is eventually reabsorbed, and with which all of creation finally coincides. The non-Christian Orient has no conception of the antinomy represented by a God at once personal and absolute, present to Himself alone in the metacosmic and intersubjective procession of Persons, inventing a world which He could have chosen not to create, and freely deciding to enter into a reciprocal relationship with it. The various Oriental doctrines have such an acute sense of metacosmic Infinity (radically illimited), of increate Eternity (surpassing all succession), of divine *Non-Duality* (something more and higher than mere unity), and of transluminous Darkness (transcending the quality of being), that they exalt these characteristics to the point of seeing in them aspects of the divine Essence itself, whereas the Biblical perspective recognizes in them, at the most, metaphysical *loci* of God's presence. The Oriental doctrines see in these concepts the divine *Quiddity* in itself, while

Monotheism recognizes in them attributes of the living God; Monotheism considers that these attributes are transcendent, necessary and absolute for us, but that they are also, nevertheless, immanent, contingent and conditioned for Him; they are " retreats " of His unknowable Essence. For the Vedic Orient, in particular, the personal God *(Ishvara)* is a mode of the metaphysical Infinite's "presence to the world, " a " determination " of Brahma; for Christianity, on the contrary, it is the metaphysical infinite which constitutes but a mode of the "presence to the intellect" of the absolute Divine Person, a metaphysical " locus " of the Holy Spirit.

Now, the living God communicates with the human person, all the more as He does not absorb, but on the contrary divinizes the person. The Hindu ascetic, once he has reached the limit of his inner withdrawal, rests therein and savors the supreme bliss of his liberating immersion in the divine infinity. But the Christian saint (and also the Hesychast ascetic), having arrived at the same point, from where the world is seen only as " dust and ashes, " invokes and calls the *Deus absconditus*, as if he were praying for the very first time : he finds that he is not at the goal, but only on the threshold of that " inexhaustible transformation " which Saint Gregory of Nyssa calls *epectasy*, and by virtue of which the saint, while receiving " the rank of prophet, of apostle, of angel, of god, " " never stops progressing " in this life, as well as " in the world to come. " Grace, far from being but a means destined to be ultimately superseded, remains for the Christian saint an End, never attained and increasingly transcendent, as it is more clearly perceived. Hesychast *theôsis*, unlike the realization of the Self, does not entail a " passage to the limit. " We would cut off the ever ascending strength of *theôsis* and " arrest " its eternally " open " movement, if we were to interpret deification as a spiritual " summation " of the divine infinity, or as a contemplative " exhaustion " of God's almightiness, considered only under its metaphysical aspect of " All-

Possibility " (the sum of what is not contradictory), or again
as an inner " leap " toward a supreme immutability, within
which there would be life or movement only in the direction
of a deterioration or descent from the contemplative summits.
Just as Origen sees in " spiritual satiety " the cause of the
angels' fall, so Hesychasm considers " Luciferian " the
aspiration after a spiritual state coextensive with the divine
Essence, a state where both the distance implied by Love and
the supraintellectual *(hyper noûn)* dimension implied by the
deifying " unknowing " of the Inaccessible, would be abolished.
For God, says Evagrius Ponticus, is at the same time the
Inaccessible and the only Intelligible : Beginning and End
of all knowing, because Unknowable; Mystery Whom knowledge
does not illuminate, because it is He Who illuminates
knowledge [2].

### The Supraintellectual Essence of Grace.

Through the supraindividual faculty of the intellect,
in particular, man does not constitute just one reflection, among
others, of the creative power, but is indeed the image of the
Creator, His final and " personal " work, His " mirror. " The
mirror, however, is not the source of light, and the intellect,
as soon as it tries to coincide with the increate Light, ceases
to reflect it. To consider the *noûs* as increate, in other words,
is tantamount to losing the conception of the increate Light
as being really communicated (but at the most symbolically)
to the intellect as such; to take this view of the *noûs* is to consider
as " innate " that Light which is nothing else but Grace : and
this amounts to cutting off the creature, at its very roots, from
Grace, i.e., from increate Love. The Greek and Latin Fathers
emphasized the created nature of the intellect, not in order
to depreciate that faculty, but on the contrary so as to open
it more fully to deification, thus protecting the *noûs*, conceived
in God's image, from the temptation to conceive of God in

its own image. " Charity, " says Saint Maximus the Confessor,
" consists in preferring the knowledge of God to everything
else; " one could say that the Luciferian temptation consists
in preferring the love of knowledge to God. In Christianity,
there is no such thing as " realization through knowledge; "
neither are there separate ways of knowledge and of love;
instead, there is the realization of knowledge through love.

In order to be thus fully " operative " and truly
" hypernoetic " (to use the Pauline form of expression), love
must have as its object a Person Who is the Absolute itself.
Since the mataphysical Orient — as we have fully explained —
does not conceive of God as personal in His absolute essence,
neither can it imagine a specific counterpart in man of the
ultimately personal God. *A fortiori*, the Orient has no idea
of the only human " reply " to God thus considered, the one
adequate " answer " of the creature to its Creator revealing
Himself as the Absolute in Person. This response is humility.
According to Saint Simeon the Theologian, Christian humility,
inseparable from the love of Christ, is the only virtue of which
man, by himself, is utterly incapable. Its essence is obedience,
and humility does not obey in order to become free from self,
but rather renounces self in order to obey. Humility, indeed,
is not a stoical disappearance into the Absolute, but a joyful
oblation to the Absolute : it is not the Gnostic auto-abolition
of self, nor even a heroic and final suppression of one's own
will, but an ever renewed abandonment of self. The " sacrificial
substance " of this oblation, far from being a destructible
or expendable object, is the individual will, which continuously
and freely wells up to feed the fire of divinizing love. In truth,
God alone can supply man with this appropriate " answer, "
and it is precisely in order fully to communicate it to man,
in order to invest man with this " reply, " irrefutably and as
irresistibly as human freedom will permit, that God personally
assumed the " form of a slave ", obedient even unto death,
and thus caused the beauty of His Face to shine forth

from the Cross, with a radiance inconceivable outside the Incarnation.

Humility-obedience — this " conformation to Christ crucified and obedient, " in the words of the Rule of Saint Basil — this virtue which is alien to Oriental spiritualities, is the keynote, so to speak, of Hesychast deification. Humility implies ceaselessly resisting our inclination to " appropriate " Grace — even on an intellective level —, i. e., our natural tendency to *autopistia* (self-confidence) and *autorythmia* (self-sufficiency). Only humility effectively surpasses man's original state and thus fulfills the Adamic vocation. Humility culminates in the supreme test (which is also unknown to the metaphysical Orient) of asceticism, " abandonment by God " : " the soul, no longer finding help in anything, even in God, " suddenly sees itself turned into an " instrument of the divine forces " (Saint Gregory the Sinaite), as if it were again — but this time " beyond all things visible and invisible " — drawn out of nothingness, recreated *ex nihilo*. That by which the ascetic felt abandoned, far from being the divine Essence, is revealed to have been only his supreme idea of it. The exceptional favor of seing the Unknowable can only be granted by being refused, as was the case for Moses, whom (in the words of Saint Gregory of Nyssa [3]) He allowed to see only His " back parts " (*Exod.* 33 : 23). Always inclined to close over its contents, intelligence can grasp the nature of the " Object " which defies every effort at definition or analysis *(aperilêpton)* only through self-renunciation, by "acceding to inaccessibility " (Vladimir Lossky).

This " unknowing " *(agnôsia)* is the complete opposite of ignorance, for it only begins at the highest limit of knowledge. To place unknowing any lower would be to injure faith and offend divine truth; but, on the other hand, to introduce knowledge beyond the threshold of the mysteries of intra-divine Life would be to empty faith and outrage this same truth. For, while it is certainly true that "contradictory" is synonymous with "impossible" on the intellectual level, all contradictions need not be resolved on that plane. And, while all opposites are indeed, at bottom, complementary in their ultimate reality, there are nevertheless some opposites whose correlation is revealed only in a supraintellectual mode, opposites which coincide only in God. These are the "divine antinomies," i.e., the mysteries of which we spoke in the Conclusion of Part I. Equipped only with the principles of contradiction, of sufficient reason and of identity, our intelligence can apprehend God only in His "intelligible concomitants." Faced with opposites which coincide beyond its own horizon, human intelligence is tempted, if not to exclude them from God as impossible, then at least to reduce them to their intellective residues. Deification, on the contrary, assumes that the whole person, touched by Grace in its preconceptual center, allows itself to be lifted up and transfigured by the very movement of the antinomies, in order to be "included" in the divine Life. It is not knowledge which clarifies the mystery; it is the mystery which clarifies knowledge [4]. The freely accepted mystery leads man to "find himself" and gain awareness on ever deeper levels of his being. The intuition of the "meeting of opposites" in the divine Essence is less a matter of the intelligence seizing God than of God seizing the intelligence : it is indeed always our true identity, our most intimate self, with which we are thus brought together again through this transforming union. Nevertheless, this identity — and Hesychast writers leave no doubt on this point — not only does not belong to us by right, but, unlike the metaphysical Self, is not considered as our sole reality, eternally underlying an illusory self; by metaphysical definition, it is not ours, but is *eternally* received. To use an expression of Saint Maximus the Confessor, it is an identity by Grace *(hê kata kharin autotês)* : the deified man becomes "without beginning" *(anarkhos)*. The increate light is truly communicated. Our God-like identity, on all levels, subsists only as far as it achieves self-transcendency, and it was by wanting to belong only to himself that Adam lost his full and true identity.

It is clear that the negative theology advocated by the Oriental Church, this " apophatic " knowledge of God, does not differ from the intellectual expression of humble and obedient love, sole means of union with the Living God of the Psalms, " Who made of Darkness his retreat. " Indeed, this God, Love in Person, remains " unknowable, " not simply because our ways of knowing are limited, but because it is of the essence of the person — and all the more of the Person — to be free, i.e., ultimately mysterious. Woe to the intelligence, says Saint Gregory Nazianzen, " which has pried into the mysteries of God " (Or. XXXI) [5]. We would say that, essentially, the person can be " met " only in and through a reciprocity which precludes coercion (action *ab extra*) and implies, on both sides, an affirmative, solemn and joyous agreement, given in complete freedom and with full assent, a " yea " which remains ever new, awesome, unexpected and unknowable. Total and reciprocal gift of self, the love of God " is exchanged " within an intersubjective interval which is continually deepening, an interpersonal space which man's unconditional " yea " converts into an infinitude of union, and his sweeping " nay " into an infernal separation.

Since the divine Person condescended to become man, it is clear that the potentialities of this " conversation " between God and man are thereby immeasurably enriched, and that the positive and negative import of this reciprocity is immensely increased by the Incarnation. Has Hesychasm drawn all the consequences attendant on the possibility of " meeting " God in the " Sacred Humanity of Christ ", and resulting from man's option to follow, shun or ignore this Humanity? At first sight, this seems like a paradoxical question, since, in the " Prayer of the Heart " or " Prayer to Jesus, " the very name of the

Saviour's humanity is the object of an uninterrupted invocation. Nevertheless, if the problem were so easily solved, Christ would not have warned us that " not all those who cry ' Lord, Lord, ' shall enter into the Kingdom of Heaven. "

Before examining this matter in the following pages, it may be advisable, once again, to raise the question which we have already propounded at the beginning of this study : why did Saint Benedict (father of Latin monasticism and, consequently, of Western civilization) not include the " Perpetual Prayer " in his Rule? He certainly knew that this prayer appeared in the Rule of Saint Basil, which in many respects he used as a model, and he had before him the famous *Collationes*, epitome of the Desert Father's spirituality, in which the monk Cassian (360-435) describes at length the perpetual invocation, in terms closely resembling those of the Hesychast treatises on the Prayer of the Heart [6]. Saint Benedict actually incorporated into his Rule many elements borrowed from the *Collationes*, which have been called " the first scientific treatise of true merit to be written on the Christian spiritual life. " Why then did he leave out the methodical aspiration to perpetual prayer? The " Messalian " turn of certain passages, for which Cassian has been criticized, does not offer a sufficient explanation, for this would have been easy enough to correct [7]. " Our prayer, " says the Rule, " ought to be short and pure, unless it chance to be prolonged by the impulse and inspiration of divine Grace " (Chap. 20). Saint Benedict does not want constant or even lengthy prayer to be systematically sought after; it should be gratuitously received. Does this mean that he shuns any method of union with God?

It is our belief that he replaced the Prayer of the Heart with another methodical and " perpetual " aspiration, namely, the ardent desire to follow the sanctifying example of Christ, not only in His prayer, but also in every aspect of His Human life. The Rule instructs the monk to follow and imitate the

God-Man in all His virtues : obedience, patience, self-abnegation, charity (Prologue, Chapters 4 and 8); to " prefer nothing whatever to Christ " (Chapter 72); " when evil thoughts come into one's heart, to dash them at once on the rock of Christ " (Chapter 4); to see in the Abbot His " representative " (Chapter 2); to salute his brothers and to receive strangers, the sick and the poor " like Christ Himself " (Chapters 36 and 53); in a word, to recognize and to meet Him everywhere, approaching every " situation " and every fellow-creature only through His intermediary. Saint Basil and Cassian had already emphasized the importance of the imitation of Christ in His humanity, but Saint Benedict was the first to recognize in this imitation the prime and " perpetual " mover of the *opus Dei*. Whether it be solitary or not, contemplative or active, union with God is always for Saint Benedict a confrontation, where interiority, thanks to the inseparably divine and human Person of the Word, is extended and blossoms in the concrete omnipresence of God. It is true that the father of Latin monasticism presents his Rule as a " modest outline " and a " primer " intended for " beginners, " but the question is precisely to find out, as we shall try to do, whether earthly life, including that of the saint, can or should be anything else than a beginning, a humble progression toward eternal life.

* * *

[1] The following considerations are not intended as an evaluation of the intrinsic reality or innermost nature of the relationship between an Oriental mystic and God, Who alone can know and judge this ultimate secret. We have in mind, in the present chapter, no so much the various Oriental spiritualities *per se*, either individually or collectively, but rather the aspects under which their influence has been effectively exercised on the majority of souls who, in the West, have earnestly turned to them. Therefore, we can now leave aside the " Bhaktic " way of Râmânuja, on which we have dwelt in Part I, a way whose goal is to realize the union of the *âtmâ* (the Self) with *Brahma* (understood as the indivisibly personal

and impersonal God), the loving knowledge of the " Lord " whose " body " consists of the entire universe, including all spiritual beings. The influence of this doctrine, which is rather close to Christianity, has remained — perhaps for this very reason — negligible in the West, as compared to that of the acosmic and *jnânic* doctrine of *Shankara*, whose goal is the intellective realization of the identity between the *âtmâ* and *Brahma* (understood as the unqualified, suprapersonal Divinity). Neither shall we take up the characteristics of Sufism, which seems to occupy an intermediate position, in many respects close to Hesychasm itself. On this subject, we refer the reader to the " Petite Philocalie de la Prière du Cœur " by Jean Gouillard (*Cahiers du Sud*, 1953, " Documents spirituels "), and to its bibliography. On the subject of Moslem esotericism, see *Du Soufisme* by Titus Burckhardt (Derain, Lyons, 1952).

² All other objects of contemplation, explains the same author, lie below the intelligence, or on its level. God alone is above it. Let us add that other " objects " (whether material or spiritual) can nourish and " satisfy " the intelligence, but that God alone illuminates it; He illuminates it, specifies Saint Gregory of Nyssa, without ever satiating it.

³ Cf. his *De Vita Moysis*, French translation by J. Daniélou (Sources Chrétiennes). By the same author : *Platonisme et Théologie Mystique* (Aubier).

⁴ On the mechanism of premature identification (either conscious or unconscious) as fundamental mode of error, cf. Balduin Schwarz : *Der Irrtum in der Philosophie*, Münster 1934. When the object of knowledge is the God of monotheism — or, generally speaking, the person —, any intellective identification is, so to say, " premature " by definition.

⁵ Is it not this characteristic of the person, at once present and mysterious — all the more mysterious, in fact, as it is present —, which Gregory Palamas also recognizes in God, when he distinguishes His inaccessible Essence from His increate and accessible Energies? This distinction would thus be real for us, but not for God. On the ensuing controversy, cf. *Palamismus und Vätertradition*, by E. von Ivanka, in *L'Eglise et les Eglises*, vol. II, pp. 29-46 (Editions de Chevetogne, 1955).

⁶ *Collatio* X, 10. It should be noted, incidentally, that the invocation or " formula " whose constant and unceasing repetition — even during sleep — is advocated by Cassian, is not the Prayer to Jesus, but the verse " *Deus in adjutorium meum intende; Domine ad adjuvandum me festina* " (Ps. 69, 2), which became the fundamental antiphon of the Benedictine Psalter, its " recurrent tonic " or keynote.

7 Starting from a rudimentary interpretation of stoical dualism, the Messalians divided the soul into a spiritual and " angelic " part, and a " material, " incurably demoniacal part. They made of constant prayer, separated from the Sacraments, the sole means of salvation; and they thought that unceasing prayer made man impeccable even in this life, while without it he would inevitably be delivered to Satan.

# 4

# Dangers and Limits
# of the Hesychast Method

The principal conclusions to be drawn from the preceding pages may be summed up as follows.

First : Hesychasm affirms the personal transcendency of God. In this, it contrasts sharply with Oriental metaphysics and, by the same token, resembles Latin theology and mysticism. It differs from the latter, however, in its origin, which is not *fallen nature* as such, but a point both superior and prior to it. Hesychasm approaches the divine Person, not from the ordinary individual self, but from its preaffective, prevolitional and preconceptual center, the heart-spirit, for " every thought will be imputed to us for sin at the last judgment " (Callixtus and Ignatius). In other words, Hesychasm approaches the divine Person on the ecclesial level of the essentially theocentric human person, which is open to the " reciprocal interiority " of beings, and not on the level of individuality, which it considers to be basically egocentric and " contractive. " This protects it at the outset from anthropomorphism in all its forms : sentimentalism, fideism, rationalism. For " God unites only with gods " (Saint Simeon).

Second : Hesychasm brings about the interiorization of consciousness — the realization of the " Kingdom of Heaven which lies within us, " the return or reversion to man's original state, the " vision of God through vision of self " — as deeply as the non-Christian Orient, from which nevertheless it differs in its goal, which is not extinction in God or realization of the " supreme identity " through knowledge, but deification through Grace, an inexhaustible and progressive ontological transmutation.

Third : Since the Hesychast synthesis of interiority and transcendency is operative and not speculative, it does not consist in reducing these two " poles " to a common conceptual denominator, but in transcending the conceptual order, while preserving the full " transforming tension " of this irreducible antinomy.

Fourth : The Hesychast synthesis assumes the existence, in man, of a point of perfection which transcends the creature without, however, coinciding with increate Grace, of a God-like faculty which is at the same time the source of the human faculties and the reflection of the divine Light. This point of perfection is the *noûs*, " mirror of God ", formless image *(eikôn aneideon)* of the Creator. It is less a matter of acquiring the *noûs* than of uncovering it and raising it from image *(eidôs)* to resemblance *(homoiôsis)*, by actualizing the potential analogy which roots nature in supernature.

Fifth : Hesychasm does not consider this synthesis as the result of a coalescence of influences or of a coordination of Eastern and Western elements, but intends it exclusively as an outcome of the Incarnation. Corollary of the Eucharistic Mystery, " which allows us to reach what surpasses nature through the very thing which is usual and natural to us " (Centuries of Calixtus and Ignatius), and of which the Prayer of the Heart constitutes the inner realization, this synthesis is not intended as the work of man, but of the Spirit of Truth active in the Church.

### *Extroverted and Introverted Techniques.*

It will be noticed that we have endeavored to describe the Hesychast method open-mindedly, and even with a degree of sympathy which will not have escaped the reader. We have felt that emphasis should be placed on one of its characteristics which does not seem to have been sufficiently stressed up to now, namely, its intermediate position between the metaphysical East and the Latin West. Spiritually as well as geographically, the Orthodox Church and Hesychast mysticism are situated at the meeting place of the two religious hemispheres.

It has been said that the Christian Church of the East is characterized, and is distinguished from the Latin Church, by the " primacy of the pneumatic and charismatic element over the hierarchical and institutional, " just as, in this view, Russo-Byzantine spirituality differs from the Latin through the " primacy of contemplation over the intellectual and active life [1]. "

Thus, the Latin mentality would be inclined to exalt " form " to the detriment of " substance. " This assertion, however, seems to raise the following question : since, on the other hand, Hesychast mysticism — which we have called an " inner liturgy " — puts much more emphasis than Latin mysticism on the technical and thus " formal " aspect of contemplation, and since the Church of the East assigns to certain aspects of the Liturgy, and hence to the ritual aspect of worship, a still more important role than does the Church of Rome — " Liturgy " means " Mass " in the Christian East —, would it not be more accurate to say that the Christian East tends, not to transcend, but rather to transfer inward this "formal, institutional, hierarchic, intellectual, active " element, to place it, so to speak, at the very center of the contemplative life? If so, this characteristic trait could be added to those which are common to Christian and to non-Christian Oriental spiritualities. Indeed, it would be a serious mistake, denoting a completely superficial view of things, to consider " technology ", i. e., systematic domination over nature, as an invention and an exclusive attribute of the modern West. Technical aptitude exists in the East as well as in the West, but while the latter prefers to direct this human tendency toward the mastery of visible nature and the harnessing of the outside world, the former, for thousands of years, has channeled it almost exclusively toward the domination of inner nature and the control of the forces of the soul. Both tendencies, when carried too far, degenerate into " technocracy, " and although it is true that an interiorized technique is spiritually more " valuable " than an extroverted one, the dangers of the former are all the greater for it.

In either case, the " automatism " inherent in any technique gradually withdraws " matter " — whether physical or psychic — from our hold, instead of allowing us to control and dominate it. While in the first instance, however, automatism threatens only our outer autonomy, in the second, our inner freedom is endangered. Indeed, an automatic spiritual activity cannot be called " free. " It is not truly willed by the person, and ceases to be " ours. " In such a case, the intimate center of the person, the ultimate core of his being, finds itself as though cut off from the inner activity " triggered " by the subject, and is thus delivered unbeknown to influences whose nature and significance largely escape our understanding.

Far be it from us to question the value of ascetic methods. In fact, the lack of any methodical control, i. e., nonobservance of the " laws " of spiritual life, is equally fatal : it cuts off from their providential end the means within our reach of drawing nearer to God, produces a passive " fideism, " and maintains the confusion, so widespread in the modern West, between the realms of the psychical and the spiritual. This is the obverse of the danger which attends overemphasis on contemplative techniques, where there exists a serious risk of mistaking the means for the end and, thus, of promoting the confusion — so prevalent in the Orient — between the ontological, natural, created order, and the spiritual, divine, supernatural, revealed order. In practice, these two extremes often alternate and coexist. Everything takes place as if the Evil One insinuated successively, and often to the same person, that all human effort is in vain, since Grace is everything — which represents the fideistic outlook — and then, the next moment, that man can do everything by himself, since he is God-like — which typifies the Pelagian attitude. Tirelessly striving to cause us to "miss" God through the propensity to extremes inherent in our fallen nature, the Archenemy thus does his best to make us swing back and forth between indolent quietism and "overexertion" of our will which, recognizing its fundamental helplessness without the support of Grace, but too "exhausted" to recover by surrendering to the divine Will, falls back onto its pillow of sloth, abandons all spiritual effort and all "technique," unless it founders in despair. The overbent bow breaks under the strain.

Hesychasm itself, moreover, offers many warnings in this respect, and it is in the spirit of its most authoritative representatives that we believe we must insist on the dangers of this method. The Philokalia often repeats the absolute necessity of following the direction of a spiritual instructor (the *staretz*). Nevertheless, the wide distribution of a book such as *The Story of a Pilgrim* [2], which summarizes in literary form the teachings of the Philokalia — allows one to assume that many of its readers undertake the "Prayer of the Heart" with neither permission nor supervision. We are thinking primarily of those who live in the world, not of monks protected by the monastic enclosure and the discipline of obedience. We have in mind the terrible disappointments which threaten those who either attempt to "savor" (or, in other words, to "appropriate by stopping there, by taking it for an end, instead of immediately offering it to God") the "sweet and luminous warmth felt in the heart," if that manifestation takes place, or, if it does not, who endlessly long for it, as though it constituted the *unum necessarium*. They forget too easily the passages where the Philokalia indignantly disavows any intention of subjecting the divine will to the automatism of the invocation, and where it specifies that these charisms, far from being a goal exempting one from works of charity, are only a means of increasing humble love. Such readers remember only the sections — numerous, it is true — which describe these gifts as the normal effect of the uninterrupted invocation of the Name of Jesus, indeed as the criterion of the " introduction into the heart " of this Name, or which emphasize the possibility of seeing here on earth the " increate Light. " This possibility is presented as exceptional — " scarcely one in ten thousand, " says Saint John Climacus —, but this very fact can arouse unhealthy ambitions which, if disappointed, produce depressions leading to agnosticism, especially if the technical adjuvants have been judged infallible.

This last point is capital. Is it really true to say, as does the most moderate contemporary Athonite writer : " None of the advocates of the Athonite technique has ever written that it was a requisite for the prayer of Jesus [3]? " Another modern Athonite, on the other hand, maintains that " one cannot pray without fasting and keeping vigil, " so that those who are unable, physically or for other valid reasons, to practice this asceticism — and there are many more such reasons today than formerly — run the risk of considering themselves as " disqualified " from true prayer [4]. Be that as it may, all the Hesychast texts in question imply that this " royal way " is especially privileged, and describe as necessary, if not the use of the interiorization technique, then at least its spiritual effects — the *charismatic* experience of the " divine answer " — in so far as this technique is practiced correctly. The reader left to his own devices is thus tempted to blame merely an improper method, or his own " technical " inadequacy, for the apparent silence of Grace, instead of recognizing in it the " silent call " by which God invites him to seek more deeply within himself, well beyond the layers of the soul which respond to a purely technical approach, for some innermost resistance to infinite

Love, a call designed to make him " hear " better God's real Answer, the reply which is to open his heart to divine depths well outside man and far beyond all charisms. Furthermore, overcome by this " divine silence " which he takes for indifference or for a refusal on the part of God, overwhelmed by the excessive reproaches which he heaps upon himself, he blames God — this " Infinite Who ignores him " — and ends by believing that there exists no infallible method of acquiring the certainty of Grace.

*The Twin Menace : Quietism and Voluntarism, Two Conjugate Extremes.*

Before attempting to solve this disconcerting problem of the " necessary " efficacy of the means of grace, it is pertinent to recall an incontrovertible fact of which the advocates of spiritual techniques should never lose sight : clearly, the Gospels contain no evidence of such " techniques. " On the other hand, they repeatedly and consistently enjoin every man born into this world to fulfill one urgent and unconditional requirement : to leave everything and follow Christ. The Scripture which more than any other exalts the infinitude of the distance between the world and God — for there is no transcendency more absolute than that of a Creator *ex nihilo* —, culminates in the Good News that this same abyss is bridged by a Love " still more infinite, " that of the God-Man " in whom dwells all the plenitude of the Divinity ". The finite being can respond adequately to the personal call of infinite Love only by his total, free, and jubilant oblation, — jubilant because this call of God in Person carries the " guarantee " that, if our offering is total, He will lend His Almightiness to the complete helplessness of the donor, and that, through the minute leverage of our immediate and unconditional oblation, we can " release " the supernatural powers of the divine Will [5].

This blessed confidence constitutes the active strength of humble Christian love and of its chief virtue, *obedience* to

Him " Who did not make avail of His equality with God, but . . .
remained obedient . . . even unto death. " One must first have
understood that " none can know by himself what is best for
him " (to quote the Rule of Saint Basil), then have trembled
with joy at the idea that His will can be done in us, in order
to accept it as a privilege " not to love one's own will "
(according to the definition of obedience given by the Rule
of Saint Benedict). To obey, adds this same Charter of Western
spirituality, is to relinquish all inner and outer " possessions, "
" instantly " and " joyfully, " without murmuring " either in
words or within one's heart, " " our hands suddenly freed,
leaving their task unfinished. " It means departing *hic et nunc*
from the very place which we occupy, i. e., where our will
now resides, whether that place be the world or a monk's cell,
the peripheral consciousness or the " place of the heart, " in
order to follow Christ. There is no other Christian criterion
of the validity and efficacy of the various contemplative methods.
Far from taking the place of obedience, a spiritual technique,
and in particular the Prayer of the Heart, is valuable only in
so far as it makes the " ear of the heart " keener and more
prompt to discern the call of Jesus in every situation, and our
innermost endeavors more submissive to the omnipotent
promptings of His Spirit of Love and Truth.

Obedience consists in doing neither more nor less than
His will. Not less, because that would fall short of total oblation;
not more — and here is the point so often forgotten today —,
because this would no longer be an oblation at all, but a
" relapse " into our own will. Thus we find again, but this time
at the very heart of the question of " technique, " the two
" currents " into which Satan, taking advantage of the " sloth
of our disobedience " at the very moment when we awaken
to spiritual life, tries to push our fallen nature : the current of
Quietism, where imperceptibly, through concupiscence, one
comes to withhold from God what He asks of us *hic et nunc ;*
and the current of Pelagianism, where, suddenly giving in

to pride, one attempts to force upon Him what He has not asked of us. We would like to show, and in so doing we are confident of interpreting faithfully the spirit of the masters of Hesychasm, how this method of prayer, in its technical aspect, thus inevitably exposes one to sin alternatively by insufficiency or by excess. To object that the aim of this prayer is precisely to withdraw the " heart-spirit, " at the outset, from the influence of these two poles of attraction is to beg the question, since this method, like all the others, can but borrow from the same fallen nature its means and its purchase or leverage.

Let us consider first the danger of insufficiency. The Hesychast method consists essentially of the solitary search for the " place of the heart " by the reabsorption of all thought into the " heart-spirit, " and of the uninterrupted repetition of the Name of Jesus in that " place, " by " adapting " one's respiration to that Name and (according to the oldest sources) holding one's breath as long as possible. This method is appealing in its ascetic simplicity. " Sit in your cell and it will teach you everything, " and " You are a temple, do not seek another place, " are two famous passages from the *Methodos*. Is there not, with the Devil's assistance, a danger of oversimplification in thus making the Christian life culminate in the repetition of the Name of Christ? It is true that " onomatolatry, " the attribution of the actual presence to the invoked Name, has been expressly condemned by Hesychasm, but the fact that it was still widespread at Mount Athos as recently as 1912 proves that the belief in the *ex opere operato* effectiveness of this invocation represents a real danger, of which some Hesychast writers, as a matter of fact, are well aware [6]. Incidentally, this tendency to " hypostasize " the name of God, so evident in Jewish mysticism and in Islam (where the Koran is often considered as increate, as " God made Word "), represents a Semitic rather than a Greek legacy in Russo-Byzantine spirituality, and one may wonder whether Moslem esoterism

(i. e., Near-Eastern Sufism) has not indirectly introduced into Hesychasm the Judaeo-Christian " incantatory " influences which Islam itself had originally received from Syrian monasticism [7]. If carried to its extreme consequences, this tendency would eventually reduce the Sacrament of the Eucharist to the purely inner and " disincarnate " invocation of the Name of Jesus. Could this possibly be why Orthodox Christians receive Holy Communion much less frequently than the faithful of the Roman Church? And does this infrequent partaking of the Sacrament denote a deep aspiration to " resurrect the soul before the body, " in the words of the Philokalia, to dissociate the spirit from its corruptible garment before death, to separate it from earthly life?

Be that as it may, every technique of invocation which is conceived of as an " inner Eucharist, " every more or less sacramental interiorization of the Rites, runs the danger of becoming an " inner ritualism " and thus of separating the spiritual from the active life [8]. To illustrate this danger, we will borrow an example from monastic life, since it is the ideal and model of Orthodox devotion : in the monasteries of the Eastern Church, the recitation of the Prayer of Jesus in the form of a rosary, accompanied by a prescribed number of inclinations or prostrations (" metanies ") " can replace all or part of the Divine Office [9]. " Noting that this formula of invocation has a virtue such that a monk can substitute it for his liturgical obligations, an ill-informed reader living in the world might easily infer, by analogy, that this daily recitation — practiced, for instance, " in the evening, for an hour or two, without interruption and in a quiet, dark place " [10] — " can also substitute for all his own duties of charity, eminently contains them, and " exempts " him from them, as it were. Believing that he has thus fulfilled his duty toward God, he will be less attentive to discern Him outside this " eminent " formula and can become insensitive to all the other infinitely varied forms of His call. Gradually forgetting that Christ always awaits him where he is, that He constantly calls him, in even the most insignificant of his daily tasks and chance encounters, his heart, indifferent to " outside " occurrences, will seek less and less to recognize the Christ Who, in and among our " least brethren, " is " hungry " or " thirsty, " " a stranger, " " sick, " or " in prison " (*Matthew* 25 : 31-46); he will then no longer distinguish His Face behind events and within his fellow man, and will perhaps give stones instead of bread to his neighbor. For Christ will answer our invocation " in the evening " only if we have answered His call " during the day. " If, on the other hand, we beg off and consider ourselves exempted from this obligation, if in the words of the parable we have " asked to be excused " by day, the one we meet and " perceive " in our nocturnal solitude may not be truly He, but only the idea we have wanted to form of God, or merely our own presence to ourselves [11].

The axiom according to which " *corruptio optimi pessima* " is particularly applicable to the Hesychast interiorization of the " Name which is above all names. " Extremely valuable when it opens the heart to the interiority of the neighbor, to the love of the image of God in the other *qua* other, and thus to the oblation to God *qua* Other, as in the case of the saints of the Christian Orient, it becomes the most dangerous snare when it imprisons within himself the invoker convinced that he is " clothing himself in Christ " by the mere contemplative " assimilation " of His Name, and in this way it induces him to withhold from " Christ in his neighbor " the " talents " which God has entrusted us with so that all of them without exception may " bear fruit. " To " hide " even one — albeit in the " abyss of the heart " — is to refuse infinite Love infinitely.

The other danger inherent in any spiritual technique, as we have indicated, is to sin by excess in wishing to offer God more than He expects. The goal of the Hesychast method is to render perpetual the prayer of the Heart, so that it may become an inner state which we have called the "Eucharist-state." This implies, as we have seen, that the real ascent toward God starts, not from fallen nature as such, but from a "point of perfection," namely the *Adamic nature prior to the Fall*, restored to its primal purity by Baptism and Penance. In the Hesychast view, this point of perfection is the "heart-spirit" (the preconceptual, preaffective and prevolitional *noûs*), and uninterrupted invocation, by converting the *metanoïa* (contrition and Sacrament of Penance) into a state, "stabilizes" the soul in its original perfection. Even assuming, however, that this "state" were attained — something which no saint has ever claimed —, would we be more protected against the Fall than was Adam? And, above all, are we not forcing upon God more than He asks of us, when we refuse to ascend toward Him from the starting point of our fallen nature? Is it not precisely for that nature, for the sick, the outcast, the sinners, and even the dead, that Christ expressly intended His act of Redemption? Has He placed on His greatest promises any *sine qua non* condition other than that of unreservedly surrendering ourselves, as we are, as He finds us, with our shortcomings, to the Almightiness of His essentially gratuitous and undeserved Mercy? To believe that we may approach Him and unite ourselves to Him only after having bathed all our wounds is to lay down our own stipulations for this required surrender, to deny Him our absolute confidence, to doubt that He alone is the author of our deifying redemption, and to deem it impossible (because insufficient) that the only co-operation expected of us be precisely this confident but unconditional surrender.

Once again, let us suppose that some of the saints did succeed in re-establishing in themselves this "original identity" with our Adamic nature, which "subsists unchanged" in the depths of our being, according to the Philokalia, although "buried beneath the passions." The mere fact of aspiring after this identity as a state cannot but defeat the aspirant's purpose, since the identity in question, as we have seen, is essentially " received. " Adam ceased to be " himself " as soon as he stopped striving to " surpass himself " in God. Consequently, to seek our Edenic nature as our " proper state " (in the words of Evagrius Ponticus) [12] implies a wish to be our own masters, and thus to repeat the same disobedience which caused the fall of Adam. The attempt to restore an " original " state both prior and superior to fallen nature, a state latent within us and which (in this view) it behooves us to bring out and stabilize through a methodical, intellectual process of interiorization *(kathastasis toû noû)*, this attempt, we say, is self-defeating since — to the extent that it seeks to turn an " infused " mode into an " acquired " condition — it reproduces the first sin, which had precisely deprived mankind of these same Adamic privileges. Taken literally, this ambition, by arrogantly encouraging us to the superhuman and futile effort of forcing them by ourselves, closes to us the gates of Paradise, which Christ has already reopened, but in a completely new way : He Himself is both the one Door and the true Initiator of our " return. " Neither is this return anything like a methodical, indeed impossible, " retracing " of the road which led us away from Eden, for one does not row up the river of time. Instead, it is the return of our fallen nature to Him, to the New Adam Who infinitely surpasses — and causes us to surpass — the Old, a return endlessly resumed and never " secured, " an uninterrupted transcendency of our entire being, including the " heart-spirit, " which also was affected by original sin. This being so, one may wonder whether repentance or " sudden spiritual change " *(metanoïa)* can become a permanent modality of our being, a " second nature " (a *metanoïa-state*), since this sudden change, on all levels, must each time find its purchase in our fallen nature, which remains fundamentally the same until our death, because its snares and temptations may endlessly alter their names, but not their basic structure. Consequently, it seems that the " Eucharist state, " which rests on the " *metanoïa*-state, " may also be an illusion. And the wish to establish the " Real Presence " permanently within us may well reflect an unconscious " self-sufficiency, " or *autorhythmia*, as this attitude is so aptly termed by the Greek Fathers. This wish, in our opinion, jeopardizes both our oblation, constantly renewed " from nothing, " which the Eucharist implies, and the ever gratuitous and inappropriable nature of this Sacrament, this medicine which always cleanses the same wounds, on all spiritual levels, even and specially on that of the saints. If it is argued that the idea of a " Eucharistic-state " is intended to make our " talents " fully " bear fruit, " we will reply that the Devil is quick to " twist " the Gospel parables so as to use them for his own ends. When we were tempted to sin by insufficiency, he suggested humility and hid from us the relevant parable of the " five talents. " Now that the sin of excess, the " Adamic " temptation to go beyond our limits, lies in wait for us (a temptation which has nothing to do with this parable), he hastens to bring up the story of the talents in order to make us forget its true moral, namely, the command to offer God all that He asks of us, to do everything in our power, but then to consider ourselves only as His " unworthy servants. "

### The Danger of Angelism.

At this point, the Devil is also careful not to remind us of the parable of the publican and the Pharisee. The word hypocrite comes from *hypokrinein*, which means both " to simulate " and " to dissimulate " and, consequently, to flaunt oneself so as " to hide " more effectively. The hypocrite hides deeply, from men, from himself, but first and foremost from God. More accurately, he dissociates his consciousness into one part which he shows, and another part which he conceals. As it persists and deepens, this dichotomy produces an increasingly intolerable split in his consciousness, since the person remains essentially indivisible. The extreme consequence of this attitude is a repressed self-hatred which inevitably leads to hatred of " Him Who created me, " a hatred whose earthly outcome can be derangement, if not mental, then at least moral (" spiritual schizophrenia "), and suicide [13].

Indeed, man knows full well that, alone, he is powerless to escape the degradation inherent in our nature. Eventually, if he refuses to make a full and explicit confession to God, he can no longer endure either God or himself. The subtle beginning of hypocrisy can be an apparently harmless feeling, namely, mere " embarrassment " or " shame " at showing God one's injuries. Instead of accepting these blemishes as " ours, " because God is absolute Love and ardently awaits this humble acknowledgement as the supreme mark of our utter confidence in Him, false shame makes us imagine God as too " perfect " to stand the sight of such defects, and suggests to us that, at bottom, they are not really " ours. "

We would not go so far as to assert that such is the origin of the Evagrian and partly Gnostic concept, according to which the ascent of the soul toward God presupposes its reabsorption into the *noûs*, restored to its Adamic purity. But we feel that such a precondition might well lead some to offer to the divine Gaze only this unsullied nature, to " wish themselves before Him " only under the highest aspect of their being, and to hide from Him their identity with its inferior aspects. Now, the determination to avoid a full, and hence personal, encounter with God can bring out a desire to consider God as other than a real Person. This is because, toward an impersonal Divinity, one may feel mistaken, but never guilty or responsible. For the opposite of impersonal Truth is merely an error, while the opposite of the Truth-in-Person is a lie [14]. Moreover, as we have explained at some length, the distance between an impersonal God and man is less absolute and more easily bridgeable by man than the " holy distance " which separates the creature from the Creator, the abyss which only He can cross, and which is not fully bridged unless He reveals Himself as infinite Person by " humbling Himself " and descending toward us. " Theopantism " (only God is real) rightly exalts the transcendency of the Divinity, in contradistinction to " Pantheism " (all reality is God). Nevertheless, an impersonal God, being only pure metacosmic Interiority, i. e., the " other side " — the nonmanifested face — of the universe, can be no more than relatively transcendent. An impersonal deity is only ontological or metaphysical, not supernatural. A Hindu may, in good faith, believe God to be impersonal, so as to reach union with Him through sheer interiorization. But a Christian can have neither sufficient reason nor real motive to conceive of God as a purely transluminous and anonymous interiority, unless it be a secret ambition, not the wish for union with Him on His terms — since He has already condescended to become united to man —, but the desire, by interiorizing Him, to unite himself with God through his own human efforts, i. e., in the final analysis, to reach Him by nature and not by Grace. There is only one more step between the pernicious refusal to assume our fallen nature and the Luciferian desire to be God by nature, a step which our arrogant pride is quick to take. And it is indeed this prideful " sadness not to be God " (in the words of Schelling) which lies in wait for us at the conclusion of the " first phase " of Hesychast deification. A method which makes of extreme " enstasy, " certainly not the summit (as in Yoga), but nevertheless the preliminary and necessary condition of the deifying union with God, inevitably makes one liable to stop on the way : it induces union only to oneself, and entails the terrible danger of self-deification. " Take heed therefore, " said Christ, " that the light which is in thee be not darkness " (*Luke* 11 : 35). Through a diabolical irony, the Prayer of Jesus " in " the heart would thus end by making a man forget to offer his heart to Jesus [15].

Many passages of the Philokalia can lead to confusion in this respect. The famous saying, " God is all the more invisible,

as He illuminates our mind more thoroughly " (Saint Simeon),
or the identification of the " naked intellect " with the " place
of the heart, " and of the latter with the " place of God "
(Evagrius Ponticus) conjure up a God Who is reducible to
a Principle of infinite interiority. The other equally famous
saying of Saint Simeon, " God unites Himself only to Gods, "
the Evagrian concept already mentioned of the " proper (original)
state of the intelligence, " and the concept of the " vision of
God through the vision of self " (Evagrius), all suggest in
man a spiritual autonomy favoring the semi-Pelagian error
which holds that the creature is entitled to Grace. With the
Devil's assistance, the transition is scarcely noticeable between
methodical interiorization, spiritual intellectualism, angelism,
and the temptation to appropriate Grace [16]. *Per se*, the concentric
movement which produces " enstasy " leads neither to the
absolute transcendency of the God-Person, nor to the complete
" self-renunciation " which this transcendency implies. We have
seen in Chapter 3 that another element is required, namely,
the sovereign initiative of God answering the unconditional
surrender of ego and " Self. " And there may be a point of
interiorization from which the " relinquishment of self " and
the " advance toward the Other " are no longer possible, if
the oblation was not total at the beginning of the recollection.
Precisely in this temptation to withhold the intelligence,
more or less consciously, from the act of oblation, may lie the
danger of an " enstasy " conceived as a first phase necessarily
preceding the second, that of the " ecstatic " leap toward the
inaccessible heights of God. Now, although it is true that the
unconditional relinquishment of self, and the total surrender
to the motions of the Will of God as Other, can and should
be initial, it is difficult to see why the movement out of self
toward the Other (" ecstasy ") need necessarily follow the
withdrawal into self (" enstasy "), and cannot just as well precede
it, if God so decides. And should such be His Will, He will
surely see to it that the immediate and unconditional " ecstatic "

surrender produces retroactively all the steps and spiritual dimensions of enstasy. The spiritual superiority of enstasy over ecstasy is eminently relative, and should not make us forget that " exteriority " is the inamissible image and support of transcendency, of the Other considered as " datum " anterior to my consciousness and my will [17]. Infinitely surpassing the " interior - exterior " opposition, God alone can determine the order in which it is best for us to experience the terms of this polarity. It is true enough that man really meets God only from his own inner depth, but it is even truer that man is not really in this depth unless he is before God. By withdrawing into myself I can, beneath the superficial and intermediate layers, find unaided the ontological core of my being; before finding my personal center, however, before discovering myself as the image of God, I must be in the presence of the personal God. To be sure, concentric withdrawal can facilitate the outward movement toward the Other, but does not *per se* lead to it. As such, " enstasy " results only in my solitary presence to myself and to the world, in the naked act of my existence in being. In the confrontation with God, on the other hand, one and the same movement of Grace awakens me to myself, impels me toward Him, and reveals to me His image in my neighbor.

In this connexion, we wish to point out that, in the Eucharistic Mystery, the believer first joins with the oblation — the sacrificial offering of His Donation, of the Victim already immolated on Calvary —, which he then receives into himself, divinized and accepted by the Father; Christ's words to the communicant that " he dwells in Me (transcendency) and I in him (interiority), " also suggest that the outward movement from self does not necessarily imply a previous introsusception. Hesychasm sometimes describes the intellect *(noûs)* as pre-conceptual, preaffective, and prevolitional, when considered as a faculty which would be ours in the " place of the heart; " but what it thus describes is not actually the intellect, however " naked, " it is the divine presence : that which is truly anterior to our concepts, to our feelings, and to our will cannot possibly be " we " or " ours, " it can only be God in us, i.e., the transforming Grace which creative and crucified Love infinitely desires to pour into " the space vacated by ourselves, " which we spontaneously offer to His redeeming Will, and this space, this act of free and total surrender, is not ours, but His.

We repeat that, in Christianity, knowledge as such is not " operative; " it is love which realizes the knowledge of God.

### Can Spiritual Effort be Necessarily Effective?

In the preceding section, we tried to show that every spiritual technique, whether Christian or not, is exposed to the vicissitudes of our fallen nature, because it cannot find elsewhere its means of action. We can now reply to the question which we had previously raised : to what extent is the effectiveness of these methodical aids necessary? This question is linked to that of the relationship between nature and Grace and, consequently, to the problem of the exact significance of the " analogy-participation " existing between creature, creation, and Creator.

The Incarnation, quite evidently, was not a necessary event, but a free and unpredictable Act. We know that God could have effected our salvation by other means, but in any case that nothing could compel Him to save us. The prophets did not " foresee " the Incarnation, and could only cryptically repeat the Mystery which God instructed them to announce. A God under compulsion from an inner necessity would not be sovereignly free. Absolutely speaking, and in the last analysis, He would therefore not be strictly a Person, but a metaphysical Principle, so that an equally metaphysical knowledge could, " in principle, " distinguish His " economy. " A " metaphysical realization " would then enable us to assimilate His nature and "put into practice" His contingent modalities of application. [18] To conceive of the divine Economy of salvation in this way would amount to reducing to a problem in comparative religion the unfathomable mystery of the Incarnation, which has precisely revealed the ultimate relationship between God and the world as the mediation of two freedoms, one sovereign, and the other received. Original sin had broken this mediation between God and man and also, because of man, between God and all other creatures. The "analogy-participation" between the world and God was distorted, as it were, through Adam's transgression and, from then on, creation was no longer spontaneously ordered to its Creator. This being so, the redeeming Incarnation could be neither the inevitable outcome of a prior historical evolution, nor the "logical" culmination of the theocentric structure of the universe. Incarnation required an unimaginable divine initiative.

Now, whereas there exists no room for a redeeming necessity or inevitability before the Incarnation, the situation is entirely different after this Divine Intervention; for this unique and unforseeable Event has taken place, the work which has reconciled us with God has become a fact, and a divine-human fact produces, once and for all, divine-human results which are indeed necessary. The cardinal and divinely simple truth of Christianity is also, strange as it may seem, one which Christians tend more and more to forget, disregard, distort or minimize. We refer to the fundamental fact that the work of our redemption is already completed, so that it is in no way incumbent on us to produce or repeat the process, but only to adhere to it. Faith, hope and charity form as many increasingly confident, joyful and unconditional degrees of this adherence. Since the act which gives us access to the divine Life is already accomplished, we are not required to deserve this act by reproducing it, but only to apply its merits to ourselves by receiving it and surrendering to it.

The Incarnation has conferred a deifying virtue on our confidence. Just as Holy Mass is the perpetually renewed oblation of a Victim immolated once and for all time, so our sanctification is the endlessly renewed consent to a Love everlastingly crucified for us. It was the confident acceptance of this Truth which strengthened the saints to the point of joyfully enduring martyrdom. Now, this consent, this adherence, this surrender, this confidence, constitute one and the same spiritual act, which depends entirely on us, and yet at the same time entails necessary spiritual consequences. We are certainly faced here with a methodical human effort, continually resumed and necessarily efficacious. This can and must be so, because the act in question, this voluntary, conscious, and constant return to the perpetual Source of our redemption, by its very nature precludes the Pelagian temptation of overestimating human effort. For methodical endeavor, in this instance, lies precisely in attributing any salutary effects not to oneself but to Christ. My will finds expression only in doing His Will; my exertions consist in relying entirely on Another for the required effort and for its results. And these same results, both natural and supernatural, for which He is pleased to credit my confident surrender, are immediately returned and " committed " to Him, through a new surrender.

Consequently, it is not proper to call the effort in question " difficult : " indeed, it proves more and more to be both impossible for us alone, and supernaturally easy with and through Christ. On the other hand, all other more or less " technical " aspects of the Christian ascetic effort are efficacious only through the mediation of that confident surrender, only in the measure that they " obey " our obedience : fasting, keeping vigil, recollection in the heart, even the uninterrupted invocation of His Name, remain completely ineffective in themselves, precisely because *per se* they are only *our* effort; in fact, their structure does not protect them against the inveterate tendency of our will to make itself autonomous.

These various techniques do not, by themselves, neutralize this hereditary desire to be our own masters, to evolve our own actions and their effects, to become " our own saviours. " It is helpful and meritorious to practice these ascetic adjuvants through obedience; but it is humbler, and thus even more helpful and meritorious, to forgo them for the sake of obedience — through submission to a concrete divine call which rules them out or simply does not call for them — knowing that they have value only as " tokens " of our absolute confidence [19]. Since nobody knows " by himself what is best for him " (Saint Basil), it is necessarily baneful to subject oneself to these exercises, for fasting and keeping vigil will then only make us lose our normal lucidity toward the countless and unforeseeable divine solicitations; in the same way, when actively pursued on our own initiative, recollection in the naked intellect and continual invocation will merely increase our propensity for self-redemption, i.e., our inclination to go no further than what Louis Gardet calls the inherent activity of " natural mysticism : " " the act of abolishing all action " or " deliberate auto-abolition of action [20]. " Its effect, says the same author, is not " sweetness and peace, " as when the Will of the Father assumes that of Christ and of the Christian, but only a " despotic mastery. " Who, in the last analysis, is the true originator of this deliberate act, which is not prompted by God? Am I still really the " actor, " at this point of " nonaction " where the ego, working its way back to its existential root, reaches its own indeterminate limits? The " despot, " in this instance, may well be he who never gives his name. Hesychasm, as a matter of fact, is fully alive to this danger. According to a work which is very highly regarded at Mount Athos, the Greek version of Lorenzo Scupoli's *Combatimento Spirituale* [21], an ascetic who mortifies himself to the utmost and who sincerely seeks, day and night over the years, inwardly to imitate the life of Christ and to assimilate His teachings, can nevertheless go completely astray, because he has unwittingly renounced everything except his own independent will. " Ways there are which to men seem right, but of which the end plunges down to the very depth of hell [22]. "

### Inner Eucharist and Imitation of Christ.

Here we approach a particularly subtle " dogmatic " danger of the invocation of the Name of Jesus interpreted as " inner Eucharist. " In the case of a monk, this danger seems to be avoided, as long as the repetition of the Name alternates with the liturgical recitation of the psalms, because the psalmody, i.e., the " sacrifice of praise, " counterbalances one-sided interiorization by an open movement toward God conceived of as the Will eternally preceding or anticipating our intuitions and our own wills. As for the layman, the risk is averted when he sees in the solitary invocation of Jesus a means of making his will prompter to recognize Him also in his neighbor. But we have seen that, for the monk, this inner invocation can replace the canonical hours, from which a layman might infer that the repetition of the Name exempts him from the duty to meet Christ in the " outer " world. The " dogmatic " danger we refer to is the error of believing that we are required, through this continuation of the Incarnation in man which (in this view) the " Eucharist-state " implies, to reproduce inwardly the very Act of the Incarnation, *to repeat* for ourselves, as it were, the divine deed of Redemption; it is the error of insisting, so to speak, on achieving by ourselves what God has already done for us once and for all, as if we wanted to be something other and more than a creature, and at the same time something other and less than a beloved son of the Creator; as if we refused to " believe, " without having first " seen, " that it is enough for us joyfully to receive the fruits of the Passion; or again, in terms of Trinitarian theology, as if a doubt regarding the meritorious efficacy of the Passion made us imagine that the Holy Spirit should proceed directly from the Father into our souls — without the mediacy of the Son — for Christ to be born in us.

This last point deserves further attention. Let us first recall that, according to the theology of the Eastern Church, which rejects the *Filioque* in the *Credo*, it is only *in divinis* that the Spirit proceeds directly from the Father, without the Son's mediation. Only in the intra-Trinitarian and purely increate order does the Spirit proceed "from the Father alone" *(ek monoû toû Patrós)*; in the order of divine interventions *ad extra* (i.e., in relation to creatures), on the other hand, the mission of the Spirit certainly takes place — as for the Latin Church — "from the Father through *the Son*" *(diá toû Hyoû)*, and not "from the Father alone." Therefore, the error which we have pointed out in connection with the inner Eucharist implies, in the eyes of the Christian Orient itself, an intolerable drifting of the increate order toward the created order or, more precisely, an usurpation by the creature of a prerogative of the Holy Spirit, to which encroachment the Church of the Orient is as much opposed as the Church of Rome. But is the former not equally opposed to the idea that the Holy Spirit "takes our place," so to speak, or again that He "stands aside, as Person, before the created persons to whom He brings Grace [23]?" Does this not amount to considering the Holy Spirit as relatively impersonal or, more exactly, as an increate Light directly accessible through an (apophatic) "negative way" dissociated from the (cataphatic) "positive way?" In other words, is the "acquisition of the Holy Spirit" — to use a phrase of Saint Seraphim of Sarov, which is often quoted in contrasting the Christian mysticism of the East with that of the West — a deification *sui generis*, a direct accession to the Trinitarian Life, bypassing the imitation of Christ's sacred humanity?

We wonder whether it is doctrinally sound, in a Christian setting, thus to dissociate the two approaches or "theologies" mentioned above: the positive or affirmative way, where man follows and meets God, in so far as He condescends to be also, though in an eminent mode, what His creatures are, in order to manifest Himself and make Himself present to them under the veil of creation; and the negative way, whereby man ascends toward God, in so far as He is not what His creatures are or can know, but remains infinitely unlike them. Does not Dionysius, the champion of apophatism, say that we can assert nothing about God, but also that we can deny nothing about Him? These two paths are certainly antinomic and apparently irreducible, in the same way as the two natures — human and divine — of Christ, but this may well be another perfect instance of those antinomies which reveal themselves to be inseparably complementary in the one and indivisible Person of the Incarnate Word. We believe that the Saints of the Christian East, as well as those of the West, followed both these paths simultaneously, precisely by conforming their entire lives, through and in the Holy Spirit, to the life of their divine Example in His humanity. Indeed, were the lives of the Saints anything else than an uninterrupted answer to the *Sequere Me* of Him Who has called Himself the Way and Who is both " the descent " of God toward the creature *(affirmatio, seu positio)*, and " the ascent " of the creature toward God *(negatio, seu remotio)* [24]? The Christian way is an encounter with God and, since moreover " the Superessential is manifested in the Humanity of Christ . . . without ceasing to remain hidden . . . in this very Humanity " — according to Dionysius himself (Epist. IV) —, this way is not only a " life *in* Christ " (Lossky, *ibid.*, p. 212), but also and at the same time a life *before* Christ, a concrete imitation of His human example.

Consequently, it seems unjustified to maintain that " the way of the imitation of Christ is never practiced in the spiritual life of the Eastern Church " (Lossky, *op. cit.*, p. 242). It was the desire to " follow Christ " and, in a very real sense, to carry His Cross which gave rise to early Christian asceticism : the first martyrs wanted to be " faithful imitations of the suffering

Christ, " because in their eyes the greatest lesson taught by the
Saviour was the Passion [25]. " The Word of God was made man, "
said Clement of Alexandria, " so that thou mayest learn from
a man how man can become God " (Protreptics, 1, 8), and
Origen, who so often likened, or even equated, the Christian
virtues to the imitation of the Saviour, " conceded that the
martyrdom of desire is not far removed from the martyrdom
of blood [26]. " What is more, Saint Basil the Great, legislator
of Eastern monasticism, states in his Rule : " The meaning
and the goal of Christianity lie in the imitation of Christ in
His humanity and according to the vocation of the individual "
(*Regula fusius tractata. Interrogatio* 43, 1, 2 : P.G. 31, 1028 BC).
Obedience deserves to be pursued for its own sake, following
the example of Christ, Who for us became obedient even unto
death, declares Diadochus of Photike a century later. And
Diadochus is not only the opponent of the Monophysites (who
consider that the divine nature of Christ has absorbed His
human nature) and of the Messalians (for whom the only means
of salvation was the perpetual, disincarnate and disincarnant
prayer); he is also, together with Evagrius Ponticus, the principal founder of Hesychasm [27].

This being so, it seems that there may be an overemphasis
on the divergence between Eastern and Western Christianity,
an unnecessary dogmatic opposition, in the insistence that,
" in Oriental Spirituality, the only way which conforms us to
Christ is the reception of Grace through the Holy Spirit, "
Grace conceived of as wholly increate (Lossky, *op. cit.*, pp. 242
and 85). As far as we are concerned, it does not appear at all
certain that, for all Eastern mystics and saints, sanctification
consists solely in " union with increate Grace, " in a " pure
ascent toward divine nature, " or that, for created persons,
this pure " ascent " precludes any " descent toward the created
being, " which " descent " could be only the exclusive
prerogative of " Christ, the divine Person " (*ibid.*, p. 212).
Would it not be more accurate to say that, for Eastern mystics

as for Saint John of the Cross and Saint Ignatius Loyola, nature and supernature, humanity and divinity, created order and increate order, interpenetrate in the transforming presence of Christ, i.e., unite without confusion, yet so intimately and above all so mysteriously, that their inamissible distinction is all the more ineffable as it is more authentically lived or experienced, and all the less expressible and expressed as its evidence more completely overthrows, confounds and heightens our understanding?

One-sided apophatism, a "pneumatism" which makes the humanity of Christ disappear into the increate Light of the Holy Spirit or, in a word, mystical Monophysism, may quite possibly represent a danger to Slavo-Byzantine spirituality, just as a one-sided "Jesuism," a certain mystical Nestorianism, threatens the modern Western outlook (cf. Footnote 4 in the Conclusion of Part I). The latter aberration, however, has not affected the saints of the West, any more than the former was the distinctive trait of the Greek Fathers, of Saint Simeon the Theologian or Saint Nilus Sorsky. All saints have followed Christ and have found in the imitation of His sacred humanity the secret of a fervor capable of rendering both sacred and holy all aspects of created life, be they sublime or lowly, central or peripheral [28]. If Eastern spirituality really gave man no share in the descent, or *kenosis*, of the incarnate Word, it would be difficult to explain how an ascetic whom the Christian East venerates as a saint, Isaac the Syrian, could have written, six centuries before Saint Francis of Assisi, that the charitable heart is "a heart which burns with love for the whole of creation, for men, for birds, for beasts . . . "

### *Limits of Analogy-Participation.*

The concept of an "inner Eucharist," whose nature and dangers we have just described, could apparently rest on the very foundation of any spiritual technique; this foundation

is the " constitutive " correlation existing between the human
" microcosm " and the universal " macrocosm " on the one
hand, and necessarily linking both these elements to the divine
" metacosm " on the other; it is *analogy-participation*. We
know that Hesychasm makes the inhaled breath (*pneuma*, symbol
of the Holy Spirit) a vehicle which carries the intelligence
toward the heart-spirit. The spiritual methods associated with
the mastery of respiration assume that, by making his the
rhythms of the universe, and through analogy-participation,
man can interiorize creation and thus rise with it toward its
increate Source. By becoming a " Christology, " which is
precisely the case in Hesychasm, this " constitutive " analogy
thus allows us to bring about, in and by ourselves, a birth
or rebirth of the God-Man, of Whom the universe, according
to Saint Paul, is the Body [29]. In this view, man is called, as it
were, to make Christ " spring forth " within himself, in so
far as He sums up or " recapitulates " all of creation. " To
clothe oneself in Christ " would thus be inwardly to " realize "
the Incarnation.

But the analogical correlation between the universe
and God, as well as between man and the universe, is not
" constitutive " of the microcosm and macrocosm; what is
constitutive is the Will of the Creator, Who is infinitely more
than a mere " regulator " of universal analogy. Although
this analogy is apparently immutable when considered *ab extra*,
it is not, *in divinis*, an absolutely necessary law, but an ultimately
contingent fact, a state of affairs which the Creator can modify
if the creature misuses it and diverts it from its Maker. We
have seen that original sin, by " deflecting " toward man the
theocentric vocation of the world, interrupted, distorted, and
impaired this vocation. Before the birth of Christ, creation
had long ceased to " culminate " spontaneously toward its
Maker, which is why, according to Saint Paul, it " groaned,
awaiting the revelation of the sons of God. " Thus Christ,
as the Universal Man, could not limit His role, so to speak,

to the " manifestation " of a pre-existing analogy-participation. He was not merely, as we have already shown, the logical and dazzling result of an " evolution " inherent in the theocentric structure of the universe. The Incarnation, in revealing infinite Love, has introduced into the relations between God and the world a new and totally unexpected dimension : the ultimately personal structure and essence of these relations. In revealing Himself as Person, He has " supernaturalized " personal values. In so doing, He has " valorized " the person to the extent of " centering " the whole universe in the element which characterizes the person, i.e., the mediation of two liberties. It is this element, and not the theocentric structure of the world — " I do not pray for the world " —, which the Incarnation has " restored, " while raising it to a new and infinitely higher dignity. Therefore, we participate in the divine Life, not by conforming spiritually to the impersonal rhythms of the universe, but by freely offering our will to that of the incarnate Creator. Hence, it is not universal analogy which makes man a " participant " in the divine order, but on the contrary it is our confident oblation to the sovereign Response of God which gives us — and through man communicates to the universe — participation in the supernatural Life [30].

Now, if we remember that the infinite " valorization " of the personal order by and through Christ has already reconciled us with the Creator, the relationship between nature and Grace becomes clearer, and we may then realize that Grace is neither " superadded " to nature, as some post-Medieval Latin theologians assert, nor " implied in Creation, " following the theology of the Christian East. Being a personal gift, Grace is not superadded, but conformed to our innermost essence. Nevertheless, Grace is not included in the continuity of the created order, because it is an unforseeable and sovereign response to our free and unconditional oblation, an ever renewed yet discontinuous encounter, taking place each time with full " consent, " between two separate initiatives. Far from being

" superadded " to our nature, it answers us in so far as we ourselves answer the Call which was addressed once and for all to mankind, and which is incessantly repeated to each man in particular. Far from being " implied " in analogy-participation, it is analogy, on the contrary, which implies Grace in order to become, each time over again, truly participant. Definitive promise of infinite Love, Grace is not arbitrarily improvised, but always lovingly given — for the Word " thirsts " for our love —; it is thus certain and " necessary " if our surrender is complete; but then, when can we really assert that our oblation was ever total? Finally, to say that Grace results necessarily, " organically, " from the methodical cultivation of our deiform structure, is to claim that we are " entitled " to what is sovereignly " gratuitous; " it is to take what can only be received, as though a beggar's outstretched hand eagerly grasped at Alms about to be proffered.

It seems to us that this is how the opposition is best resolved between the two " viewpoints " described at the beginning of this study, in connection with the relationship of nature and supernature; namely, the viewpoint of the Christian Orient, which sees in the " nature " of man only the image of God *in posse*, and that of some Latin theologians, who seem to reduce this nature to the " law of sin. " Actually, these are not two distinct conceptions, one of which must be true and the other false, but rather two aspects of the same indivisible person, two tendencies or " moments, " one deiform and the other deifugal. Both conceptions are accurate, but by turns, as, on the threshold of any action (either inner or outer), we actualize one or the other; as, starting from the innermost root of the free act, we choose fallen nature or nature restored by Grace. It is an inescapable and ever-present choice; to evade it would be to act without passing through the personal center of our being, to deprive our actions of the divine-human sanction which alone makes them both free and ours, and thus, to choose fallen nature in advance. We are always seeking to avoid this

free choice, however, less because it is difficult than because
it is painful for our pride and concupiscence thus constantly
to return to that central point of our consciousness where
— we know it full well — our indigence before the Creator
and our responsibility as His creature are clearly evident [31].
Another way of escaping this choice is to view these two natures
" in space, " as two superposed levels, so as to be able to
" realize " the higher level (redeemed nature) by freeing oneself
from the lower (fallen nature). Such a bisection of the person
is both unrealistic and misleading; the person is in fact indivisible;
it is always the whole person which stumbles and rises again.
As long as we live on earth, the answer to the question whether
Grace fulfills or contradicts nature finally depends on our
response to Grace. The alternative is inexorable and absolutely
the same for every Christian. On this point, as on so many
others, it is vain to set in opposition the Churches of Rome
and of the Orient.

### Conclusion : Value of the Hesychast Method.

The preceding pages lead to an explanation of a fact
which at first sight appears paradoxical, namely, the profound,
persistent and today unquestioned influence which Evagrius
Ponticus has exercised over all Hesychast spirituality, although
he was anathematized by two Ecumenical Councils for his
" Origenism. " Evagrius certainly seems to be the actual author
of Saint Nilus' famous " *Treatise on Prayer;* " Saint John Climacus
opposes certain points of his doctrine, but elsewhere calls him
" messenger of God " *(theôlatos) ;* Saint Maximus the Confessor
criticizes him severely, while incorporating most of Evagrius'
ascetic doctrine into his own work [32]; and the Philokalia
reproduces, under different names, more than one aphorism
of the inspired ascetic of Scete. Now, Evagrian doctrine clearly
gives the specifically " Oriental " mode of spirituality, which
seeks pure interiorization, precedence over the Monotheistic

and especially Christian mode, which is centered completely on absolute transcendency. It is this precedence of the first mode that the Church has condemned, because, as we have tried to show, it tends to absorb the second, even in the attenuated form of a methodical and necessary priority of " enstatic " recollection over the " ecstatic " leap toward the inaccessible heights of God. But the Church has not rejected Evagrius' work as a whole; because Hesychasm " clandestinely " gathered and transmitted the penetrating views of the disciple of the Cappadocians on the contemplative " stripping " of the intelligence on the threshold of the Trinitarian mystery, we are today in a better position to appreciate the value and gauge the dangers, in a Christian setting, of the identification of the " place of the heart " with the " naked intellect " in its " Adamic purity. " By preserving the legacy of Evagrius, Hesychasm has prepared the way for a true spiritual dialogue, now sorely needed, between East and West.

Besides, the dangers which we have mentioned allow us to understand why Hesychasm, since the beginning of the last century, has tended more and more toward " a complete separation between the prayer of Jesus and the psycho-physiological techniques [33]. " In the words of the last edition of the Philokalia, which we owe to the Russian ascetic Theophanus the Recluse (1815-1894), " One must remember that our only contribution is in striving, whereas reality itself, i. e., the union of the intelligence and the heart, is a gift of Grace, bestowed *when and as the Lord wills* [34]. " If the strictly technical devices of Hesychasm are thus put back into their proper place, and are dissociated from the heterodox conceptions from which, in part, these devices stem, or to which they themselves have sometimes given rise, then the Hesychast method can regain its full value without spiritual dangers. We see this value especially in *Hêsychia* itself, which means " peace, rest, tranquillity, " and in the inner effort which the Philokalia constantly advocates in order to reach it : the immediate rejection

of every thought which is foreign to the content of the
invocation "Lord Jesus Christ, Son of God, have mercy on
me!" Recently, a contemporary Athonite monk has rightly
insisted on the truly fundamental role, at the beginning of
the Prayer and of our actions, of this instantaneous rejection,
before a thought or an intention other than the humble appeal
to the Lord "can take shape[35]." Consequently, the goal of
this ascetic effort can be neither self-mastery, nor attainment
of a spiritual "state," nor again escape from the world —
"I do not pray that Thou take them out of the world, but that
Thou keep them from evil" said the Son to the Father in
instituting the Eucharist, — because the cause of this effort
is not within ourselves. Our striving proceeds entirely from the
peaceful and blessed certainty that we are, here and now, the
objects of infinite Love, and its goal is to make this Love shine
in us and from us in the selfsame way that we received it:
serenely, joyfully, and freely. Continually breaking in upon
the indolence or pretentious autonomy of our fallen nature,
the confident and constant return to the "place of Peace,"
far from dividing our consciousness by dissociating it from
our daily life, unifies it to the point of making us recognize
in each one of our fellow creatures a messenger of the Lord,
and of transforming every situation into a jubilant sacrifice
of praise. All this requires further definition.

It can never be overemphasized that progress in the
Christian spiritual life is diametrically opposed to the Gnostic
ascent. Christian progress is not measured by the gradual
abolition of lapses and imperfections, but by the increasing
rapidity with which one recovers from them; sanctity consists
much less in not falling, than in recovering so fast that,
*ultimately*, the return to God coincides with the "relapse"
or, to be more accurate, with each deifugal movement of our
fallen nature. Seen from outside, the saint appears, because he
is impeccable, much less exposed to temptation than other
men; seen from within, however, he is actually much more

exposed, because he does not hide any temptation from himself and immediately experiences as sins a thousand lapses which the average believer takes for harmless tendencies " still within the straight path [36]. " The saint is thought of as impassible and strong, to the point of being able to ignore the vicissitudes of our fallen nature. Actually, he is lucid and humble, to the extent that each symptom of his weakness, far from disturbing, discouraging, or depressing him, instantly rekindles in him the blessed certainty that by himself be can do nothing, but that with God everything comes within his reach. It is the recollection of this truth which the saint has made " perpetual, " and the prayer of the heart is fully Christian only in the measure that it contributes to actualizing this recollection, on the occasion of each inner or outer impulse. That which the saint has conquered, and which we must overcome, is much less temptation *per se*, than the subtly prideful tendency, caused by temptation, temporarily to do without God. This habitual result, this " postponement " of our recollection of the Redemption, is thus a manifestation of our secret ambition to do " everything " by ourselves and nothing through God, at least for a time and in some corner of our soul. The same evidence of our complete beggarliness, which insensibly isolates us from God and engulfs us in our weak and wretched autonomy, joyously leads back to the power of the Saviour those who " glory in their weakness. "

The Gnostic ascent begins with a solitary striving after liberation, with an autonomous activity directed toward the abolition of action, and its end is a peace conceived of as non-active independence, an aspiration latent in many Christians. The ascent of the saint, on the other hand, begins with peace, a peace received from God and resulting entirely from a firm adherence to the preaccomplished Redemption, and its end is the ever more freely willed, and thus ever more active surrender to perpetually transforming Grace. The saint never ceases, here on earth, to " return, by the labor of obedience, to Him from Whom he has strayed through the cowardliness of disobedience. " Only in eternity, of course, does this peace become totally active; resurrection, which is a deliverance from all hereditary sloth, a full flowering of the person *in conspectu Dei*, far from abolishing our free and vivifying " answers " to the Source of Life, multiplies them infinitely.

Let us now consider this constantly renewed return and recourse to the merciful Almightiness. Are these elements not precisely the content of the Prayer of Jesus? The dangers and errors pointed out above exist only, in fact, when and to the extent that the " letter " of this prayer prevails over its " spirit, " i.e., the incantatory formula over the humble, lucid, and ardent appeal, the state of intellectual interiorization over the intimate and total oblation, the spiritual " reflex " over the ceaselessly renewed supernatural impetus, " spontaneous " automatism over the initiative originating in the personal center. Since (as we have seen) human nature remains fallen, even in a saint, and since the elect remains forever a creature eternally and sovereignly vivified by the Living God, it is clear that perpetual prayer, in order to be truly Christian, must be something else and something more than a sort of " theocentric reflex " of the heart, or a habitual sacralization of the consciousness which has become a " second nature. " Habit and freedom, reflex and love are mutually exclusive terms; the saint is not a sacred animal.

On the other hand, when fused with and subordinated to the " spirit " of this prayer (as we have just described it, and as it has been considered by all the saints of Hesychast affiliation), the " letter, " instead of being a dangerous obstacle, in turn acquires a vivifying virtue of its own. The Hesychast method then becomes extremely valuable in making us really vigilant, in the evangelical sense of the word. Everything we have said of impassiveness *(apatheia)*, of the " remembrance of God " *(mnêmê toû theoû)*, of the inner fight against our " tendency to take illusion for reality " *(planê* or *prelest)*, of repentance as a sudden intellectual change *(metanoïa)*, when stripped of all Gnosticism, effectively supplements the data of Eastern and Western spirituality, both ancient and modern, on the discernment of spirits. Indeed, these various concepts afford as many ways for us to discover more and more quickly the movements of the soul which imperceptibly remove us from the " place of Peace, " the movements which the " demons lurking somewhere about the heart " persuade us to confuse as long as possible with inspirations from on high. But it is a mistake to demand more from a method than it can give, and a Christian spiritual technique cannot be more than an element of the " co-operation, " at once infinitesimal and essential, which God expects in order to gratify us quite differently and infinitely more than we can possibly foresee.

As for " concentric " recollection in the " place of the heart, " the main point is to avoid separating this phase, even for a moment, from the confrontation with God. It has been pointed out that we can find our ultimate depth only before God, i.e., through this confrontation. Therefore, every informed spiritual director will see to it that this " meeting " always accompanies or precedes the " descent of the intelligence into the heart; " failing which, there is real danger that the latter might carry one gradually toward an ontological solitude cut off from the supernatural Source [37]. Practiced under a direction which saves it from this danger, methodical recollection in the depths of the heart can and should, on the contrary, help admirably to submit more and more our least actions, including our intellectual activity, to the " sanction " of the free and deiform center of our person. Thus conceived, concentration in the heart does not constitute an invitation to " transcend " the interior-exterior polarity, but to *unify it*, to integrate it in the personal plenitude of the free act. Far from Gnostically isolating the deepest level of the soul from its intermediate and peripheral levels, this concentration links the innermost center to them and makes it shine in all the movements of the soul, in all the gestures of the body, and through the body, into the heart of one's neighbor [38]. It is not the least of Hesychasm's merits forcefully to have recalled the dignity of the body as temple of the Holy Spirit and as " epitome " of the universe, or " microcosm; " provided, however, the prefix of this last word — so often misunderstood — does not make us forget that, in reality, the " macrocosm " is ordered to the " microcosm, " which alone is in the personal image and resemblance of God, and not merely His sign or trace. The quantitative minuteness of man only emphasizes the immeasurable qualitative value of the person, whose supernatural splendor shines forth from the inner face of Christ and the Saints. The universe can be conceived of as sacred, but only the person can be holy [39].

The real tragedy of the modern world, writes Heidegger, is to have lost the sense of the sacred. Our only real tragedy is not to be saints, said Léon Bloy. In our opinion, the sense of the sacred — i.e., transparency to the metacosmic Light —, together with interiority, which is inseparable from it, seems to be the eminently Oriental spiritual dimension; we believe that holiness — full participation in the personal Life of God —, and the absolute transcendency which it implies, constitute the spiritual dimension which is specifically Monotheistic, and peculiarly Christian.

Situated in the geographical and spiritual borderland between the world's two religious hemispheres, Hesychasm quite naturally found itself led to incorporate into Christ both of these " dimensions " or components, and represents the first attempt to integrate into God-made-Man all the essential features worn throughout the world by man's striving toward God. It seems that Hesychasm has thus opened the way which it is incumbent upon us to follow, at this moment when, for the first time in history, East and West interpenetrate over the whole surface of the earth.

\* \*
\*

[1] *Un Moine de l'Eglise d'Orient*, op. cit., p. 34.

[2] English translations by Dom Theodore Bailey : *The Story of a Russian Pilgrim* (London 1930), and by R. M. French : *The Way of a Pilgrim* (London 1930). German and French translations have also been published.

[3] *Un Moine de l'Eglise d'Orient*, op. cit., p. 72.

[4] Here is the passage in question : " While *vigil*, carried to the limits of individual endurance, endows the intelligence with a keenness and a clarity unknown without it, fasting recalls man to himself, helps him to bring his being into coincidence with the limits of his body, and the asceticism of thirst is one of the conditions necessary to progress in inner prayer . . . : one cannot pray without fasting and keeping vigil . . . " (Hieromonk Antoine Bloom : *L'Hésychasme : yoga Chrétien?*, loc. cit., p. 181). We will also quote the following advice from an unchallenged authority in the Eastern Church, Saint Seraphim of Sarov (1759-1833), taken from his justly famous *Conversation with Motovilov* : " In order to receive and *feel in the heart* (the italics are ours) the light of Christ, one must withdraw as far as possible from all visible things. When the soul, with an inner trust in the Crucified, has been cleansed by penitence and good works, one must close the bodily eyes, cause the understanding to descend into the heart and incessantly call the Name of Our Lord Jesus Christ : ' Lord Jesus Christ, Son of God, have mercy upon me! ' Then man, in proportion to his zeal and to the attachment of his spirit to the Beloved, finds in the invocation of the Name, a delight which awakens in him the will to seek the highest illumination. " (Quoted in *Un Moine de l'Eglise d'Orient*, op. cit., p. 78).

[5] Cf. the famous " Ignatian Maxim " : " Make this the first rule of your actions : Rely on God as if the success of the undertaking depended entirely on you and not at all on God; nevertheless, do all your work as if nothing depended on you and all on God. " For Saint Ignatius Loyola, nature and supernature interpenetrate through and since the Incarnation, or more exactly : life in the Incarnate Word endows man with the ability to actualize this interpenetration by concretely surrendering his will to the divine Will, which the *Spiritual Exercises* teach us precisely to recognize *hic et nunc*. It is only later that one came to separate nature and supernature, to the point of attributing to Saint Ignatius the statement that natural means can produce but natural results, and that only supernatural means (e. g., the sacraments) produce supernatural effects. See Gaston Fessard's brilliant analysis of this distortion of Ignatian thought : *La Dialectique des Exercices spirituels de Saint Ignace de Loyola* (Paris, Aubier 1956), pp. 305 ff.

[6] For example, *Un Moine de l'Eglise d'Orient*, op. cit., p. 84.

[7] See Thor Andrae's *Mohammed* (1918) and *The Origin of Islam and of Christianity*. (Upsala, 1926).

[8] I. Hausherr points out that the state of pure intellectuality *(katastasis noós)* obtained by the exclusion of every concept, is " still pre-eminently a state, not because of its long duration, but because it excludes deeds. " (*Revue d'Ascétique et de Mystique* : " Comment priaient les Pères, " January-March 1956, p. 51). By the same author : *La méthode d'oraison hésychaste*, in *Orientalia Christiana*, Rome, Vol. IX (1927), No. 36; and *L'Hésychasme, étude de vie spirituelle*, ibid., Vol. XXII (1956), pp. 5-40 and 247-285.

[9] *Un Moine de l'Eglise d'Orient*, *op. cit.*, p. 69, and the note showing the table of equivalences.

[10] Following the recommendation of Nicodemus the Hagiorite's " *Manual* " (pub. 1801) quoted *ibid.*, p. 63.

[11] On the subject of pure actuation of the " I " as a typical end-result of non-Monotheistic forms of mysticism, see note 22 below.

[12] Evagrius calls this original identity *arkhikê katastasis*, " primordial state. "

[13] On the subject of Pharisaism and its secondary manifestation, self-righteousness, see Dietrich von Hildebrand's *True Morality and its Counterfeits* (New York, David McKay, 1955), which is the second volume of his trilogy on Christian Ethics.

[14] On this subject, see *L'Eternel dans l'homme*, by Max Scheler, and *La Pensée hébraïque*, by Claude Tresmontant.

[15] Some ascetic advocates of " Origenian " realism went so far as to call themselves *isokhristoi*, " equals of Christ. "

[16] Through true " orison, " writes Evagrius, the monk becomes *isangelos*, the equal of angels (*De Oratione*, p. 113). For Evagrius, this does not simply call for a certain mood or state of soul, but rather for a really different state of being (cf. Hausherr, *loc. cit.*, p. 48). The object of Evagrian spirituality is to reach, in this life, a supraterrestrial level of existence, freed of the limitations — and thus also of the requirements and obligations — of our human condition. This ambition to become pure, nonactive intelligence certainly constitutes " Angelism, " and the wish to recover this status is a clear case of " Origenism. "

[17] The " inside " is no less " spatial " then the " outside " or the " above, " writes Henri de Lubac (*Sur les Chemins de Dieu*, Paris, Aubier 1956, p. 113). " I cannot help fearing that this cult of interiority may after all be an inverted spatial prejudice. " (Gabriel Marcel, quoted *ibid.*, p. 300).

[18] On this subject, see René Guénon, *L'Homme et son Devenir selon le Védanta*, Paris, Chacornac.

[19] " It is more meritorious, said Saint Teresa of Avila, to pick up a needle in obedience than to eat and drink nothing but bread and water for a whole year. "

[20] " Recherches sur la Mystique Naturelle, " *Revue thomiste*, 1948, No. 1-2, p. 98.

[21] Cf. the English translation of the Russian version, by Kadloubovsky and Palmer, under the (Athonite) title : *Unseen Warfare* (Faber & Faber, London.) *Combatimento Spirituale*, by the Catholic priest L. Scupoli, was published in Venice in 1589. His source certainly seems to have been the *Arte de servir a Dios*, a work which was well known at the time of the Franciscan Alonso of Madrid, first published in 1521. On this subject, see Fidèle de Ros, *Revue d'Ascétique et de Mystique*, April-June, 1954.

[22] *Prov.* 16, 25, quoted in the Rule of Saint Benedict, Chapter 7. The height of " natural " mysticism, as Louis Gardet rightly points out *(op. cit.)*, is not the accession to pure being, but pure actuation of the " I " in being. Now, in a Christian setting, such an " isolation of self " (the Hindu *Kaivalya*), far from leading *per se* to God, constitutes as such an isolation from God. Since the whole of mankind is affected by original sin, and since our nature is thus never " pure nature, " we prefer to call " non-Monotheistic " the schools of mysticism which Louis Gardet calls " natural. "

[23] Vladimir Lossky, *Théologie Mystique*, p. 169.

[24] On the subject of the *via positiva*, the *via negativa* and their synthesis in the *via eminentiae vel transcendentiae*, we recommend the profound and perceptive comments of Henri de Lubac in *Sur les Chemins de Dieu*, pp. 144 ff. This intellectual, or rather transintellectual and contemplative synthesis is existentially achieved by the Saints, who assume the life and death of the Risen Christ, and share His humiliations (His " *kenosis* "), as well as His Transfiguration.

[25] See in *Dictionnaire de Spiritualité Ascétique et Mystique* the article entitled " Ascèse, " Section IV, Beauchesne, 1955, col. 964.

[26] *Ibid.*, col. 965.

[27] See his *Cent Chapitres sur la Charité*, Chap. XLI, and the Dictionary mentioned above, fasc. XX-XXI (1955), col. 832.

[28] In a recent article entitled "Christ and his Church," which has just come to our attention, the distinguished Russian theologian George

Florousky also wonders whether Vladimir Lossky does not carry too far the distinction between the " Economy of the Spirit " and the " Economy of the Son. " Mr. Florousky, it should be noted, considers the question from an ecclesial and not a mystical point of view. " The implicit idea (of Mr. Lossky) seems to be that only in the Spirit, and not in Christ, is the human personality fully and ontologically rehabilitated. . . . " " Now, is not the relationship with Christ, established and maintained ' through the sacraments, ' precisely personal — a personal encounter —, and is it not accomplished through the Spirit? . . . " " It is dangerous to ascribe to Christ only the ' organic ' aspect of the Church, its ' accent of necessity, ' and to attribute to the operation of the Spirit the ' personal ' aspect of the Church, its ' accent of liberty. ' " (*L'Eglise et les Eglises*, Editions de Chevetogne, 1955, Tome II, pp. 168-169).

[29] According to Saint Paul, that which forms the universal body of Christ is the union of the faithful in the Church (*Rom.* 12 : 5; I *Cor.* 12 : 27), and the cosmos only through participation in the Church (*Rom.* 8 : 19-22; I *Cor.* 15 : 39-41). On the tendencies of Russian theology to identify the Church with the " cosmic body " of Christ, cf. Lossky, *op. cit.*, p. 107, and his refutation of these tendencies.

[30] Analogy always implies a certain proportion, hence a necessary relation. Between the world and God, between the highest human intelligence and the Creator, the disproportion is infinite. Analogists, i. e., those who try to carry analogy beyond its reasonable limits, are well aware of this. But what they fail to recognize is that the disporportion in question grows larger as the correlation becomes more evident, that the " dissimilarity " between the created and the Increate increases at the same time as the " similitude. " The human mind seems to be more " analogous " to the divine Spirit than is the physical sky to the super-natural heaven; in actual fact, the dissimilarity, discontinuity, or " distance " is still more immeasurable between the former than between the latter.

As for " inverse analogy, " as René Guénon sees it, between the metaphysical finite and Infinite, this concept still constitutes an " apophatic " proportion, though a negative one. Through the mediacy of metaphysical knowledge, inverse analogy indirectly reintroduces between man and God the elements of commensurability or continuity which it seemed originally to deny, and thus attributes to God an inner necessity which would be negatively accessible to our knowledge, or rather to our " unknowing. " We fail to see of what help inverse analogy could be with respect to God's self-revelation as Person, or with respect to the Trinity and the Incarnation, for example.

Although enlightening within its providential limits, analogy — whether direct or inverse — becomes a source of confusion when it exceeds those limits. In the latter case, analogy shuts itself off from reality, and dissolves the intelligence in the darkness of impersonalism. The great danger of analogism is to make us lose our spontaneous attitude before what is most present and most incomprehensible to us : the tremulous sense of wonder, this " response " sent by God into the soul in order to reveal Himself therein as He " Who is above me, not as the sky is above the earth . . ., but because He has created me " (Saint Augustine).

[31] Therefore, repentance in the sense of " sudden intellectual change " *(metanoïa)* is efficacious only if it is preceded by moral repentance. It cannot possibly exempt one from the latter by replacing it, since *metanoïa* is a result of moral repentance, which, being always a free and new step, obviously cannot become a " state. "

[32] On this subject, cf. M. Viller : " Aux sources de la spiritualité Maximienne. Les Œuvres d'Evagre le Pontique. " *Revue d'Ascétique et de Mystique,* April and June, 1930. Also, I. Hausherr : *Le traité De Oratione d'Evagre le Pontique, ibid., XV,* 1933.

[33] *Un Moine de l'Eglise d'Orient, op. cit.,* p. 80.

[34] Quoted, *ibid.,* p. 80. According to the same great master of Orthodox spirituality, the classical methods of Hesychasm have, " as a general rule, become superfluous in their Athonite features, and constitute a danger for novices without a teacher, for such methods might, in these beginners, take the place of the spiritual work itself . . . " (Hieromonk Antoine Bloom, *op. cit.,* p. 194).

[35] Hieromonk Sophrony : *Des Fondements de l'Ascèse orthodoxe,* Paris, 1954, pp. 26 and 55.

[36] At this point, it may be opportune to recall once again the following passage from the Rule of Saint Benedict : " Ways there are which to men seem right, but of which the end plunges down to the very depth of hell. " *(Prov.* 16 : 25).

" Although the saints are those who have nothing more than imperfections to reproach themselves with, ' for example, if, possessing several supernatural lights on a subject, they were to choose the lowest, through weariness of spirit or thoughtlessness ' (P. Lallement, *Doctrine Spirituelle,* p. 242), it is they who best realize the opposition of Grace and sin. Therefore, they feel the greatest terror of the judgments of God, although their salvation is ' morally certain ' *(ibid.,* p. 452). For ordinary morality, which is both abstract and objective, not to choose the best means to be satisfied with the lesser good. On the contrary, in the concrete, intimate and subjective judgment of the saints, such an option is seen increasingly as the choice of the worst. " (Gaston Fessard, *Dialectique des Exercices Spirituels de Saint Ignace*, p. 56).

[37] On the subject of Spiritual Direction in the Christian Orient, particularly among the Desert Fathers, see the authoritative article by I. Hausherr in the *Dictionnaire de Spiritualité Ascétique et Mystique*, Fasc. XXI, pp. 1008-1060. The analysis of *diakrisis* (discernment of the deifugal or deiform powers of the soul), of *nepsis* (attention), and especially of *exagoreusis* (the opening of the soul to one's " spiritual Father ") is most informative. One finds here the foundation of all subsequent spiritual methods, including that of the *Exercises* of Saint Ignatius Loyola.

One must " dash at once on the rock of Christ the evil thoughts which come into one's heart, " says the injunction quoted above (p. 114) from the Benedictine Rule, and it adds : " . . . and manifest them to one's spiritual father " (Chapter 4.) According to the desert tradition, it is enough to write of an evil thought to one's spiritual father, for it to be dispelled. *(op. cit.)*

[38] This integration of all the modalities of consciousness reaches perfection in the saint. We are tempted to see here a temporal progression toward the beatific state where " God shall be all in all. " Recalling his rapture to the third heaven, Saint Paul writes : " Whether it took place in the body or out of the body, I know not. " These words seem to indicate that, in rapture, " enstasy " and " ecstasy " constitute a biunity without confusion or separation.

[39] Regarding the " saint, " as he transcends and integrates the " sacred " (the *numinous*), cf. Dietrich von Hildebrand, *Graven Images*, David McKay, New York, 1957. " Upon meeting a saint, " says Henri de Lubac, " it is not an ideal, already formed within us, which at last we find realized and lived out . . . The wonder is of a different order . . . It is like a new ' homeland, ' at first unknown to us, but immediately recognized as being older and truer, which claims our heart. " (*Sur les Chemins de Dieu*, p. 182).

Printed in Belgium by DESCLÉE & Cie. ÉDITEURS, S. A., Tournai — 10.417